DEAR OLD ROSWELL

DEAR OLD ROSWELL

Civil War Letters of the King Family

of Roswell, Georgia

Edited by

T. H. Galloway

Mercer University Press
Macon, Georgia

ISBN 0-86554-811-0
MUP/H614

First Edition.

∞The paper used in this publication meets the minimum requirements of American National Standard for Information Sciences—Permanence of Paper for Printed Library Materials, ANSI Z39.48-1992.

Library of Congress Cataloging-in-Publication Data

Galloway, T. H.
Dear old Roswell: Civil war letters of the King family of Roswell, Georgia / edited by T. H. Galloway.
1. King, Barrington S. (Barrington Simeral), d. 1865—Correspondence.
King family—Correspondence. 2. Confederate States of America. Army. Cobb's Legion—Biography. 3. Georgia—History—Civil War, 1861-1865—Personal narratives. 4. *Roswell* (Ga.)—Biography. 5. Virginia—History—Civil War, 1861-1865—Personal narratives. 6. United States—History—Civil War, 1861-1865—Personal narratives, Confederate. 7. *Roswell* (Ga.)—Social conditions—19th century. 8. Georgia—History—Civil War, 1861-1865—Social aspects. 9. United States—History—Civil War, 1861-1865—Social aspects. I. Title.

E605 .D43 2003
973.7/82 22

2003016022

Contents

PREFACE

The Civil War has captured the imaginations of historians and history buffs alike for more than a century. Although numerous works have been produced on the Civil War, this interest and fascination is best satisfied through the examination of original documents, such as correspondence, that serve as firsthand accounts. A set of letters written by a family as they experienced the war often supplies the details of the battles and of soldiers' experiences as well as the daily lives of those left at home. By reading the actual correspondence, the reader is captivated and transported to that time, seeing the war through the eyes of soldiers and their families.

This general interest in the Civil War and the information available through letters leads us to examine the King family of Roswell, Georgia. The King family, spread between Roswell and Virginia, faced the perils of war on many different fronts. The material covers Barrington S. King, a lieutenant colonel in Cobb's Legion, leaving his home in Roswell, Georgia, to fight in Virginia. On the other end of the correspondence are his father, mother, and young son in Roswell. Between the lieutenant colonel and the family in Roswell is his devoted wife, Bessie, who followed her husband to Virginia and traveled between the front and Roswell periodically, providing a woman's view from near the front as well as from home.

The correspondence covers the investments of the members of the King family; their company, the Roswell Manufacturing Company, which manufactured cloth for the Confederacy; the death of friends and a brother in the war; and the refugee experience of those fleeing Northern advances on Atlanta. Since Barrington S. King was an officer, his experience in the Civil War differed from the experience of privates. His financial status enabled him to live at a level of moderate comfort during the war.

This set of letters is remarkable because many of Bessie's and Barrington's letters survive, providing different perspectives of the same incidents. Also fascinating are the details of Jessy, the trusted family slave, who followed the young King to Virginia and escorted his wife around the Southeast throughout the war. In addition, the letters give accounts to what took place when the Union forces occupied Roswell, including the opening of Roswell King's burial vault, a secret Bessie kept from her husband's relatives.

Lieutenant Colonel Barrington Simeral King was the son of Barrington King and Catherine Margaret Nephew.[1] His grandfather, Roswell King, who founded Roswell, Georgia, was the former overseer of the estate of Pierce Butler, a slaveholder on St. Simon's Island most notably portrayed in the famous antislavery diary of his wife, Frances Anne Kemble, *Journal of a Residence on a Georgia Plantation in 1838–1839.* Another notable extended family member was his uncle, Thomas Butler King, who was a member of the Georgia legislature, the US House, and Georgia's official envoy to the courts of Europe. Although these family members are not included in this collection of letters, their connections and status demonstrate the importance of the family in the region.

The King family relocated from the Georgia coast with five other families to found Roswell 20 miles north of what later became Atlanta. Roswell King discovered the area just north of the Chattahoochee River while surveying for gold as a representative for the Bank of Darien. Enjoying the landscape where Cedar (Vickery) Creek dumps into the river, King established a

---

[1] Catherine Margaret Nephew, daughter of James Nephew and Mary Magdalen Gignilliat, was from McIntosh County, Georgia.

community that would combine industry and agriculture while allowing its residents to live as devout Presbyterians.

The letters have been transcribed, retaining original word usage, punctuation, strikethroughs, and abbreviations. This allows the reader to better understand the people who wrote these letters and provides the feeling of reading the originals. Underlining has been replaced with italics. When necessary, footnotes explain a comment, clarify a meaning, or give background information. Also added is general Civil War information regarding Cobb's Legion. Except where noted, all soldier identifications are from Janet B. Hewett, ed., *The Roster of Confederate Soldiers, 1861–1865,* vol. 16 (Wilmington NC: Broadfoot Publishing Company, 1995). The original letters are housed in the Library/Archives of the Atlanta History Center, where they are available to the public.

Barrington King

Catherine Margaret
Nephew King

James Roswell King

Captain Barrington
Simeral King

Captain Thomas
Edward King

Barrington Hall.

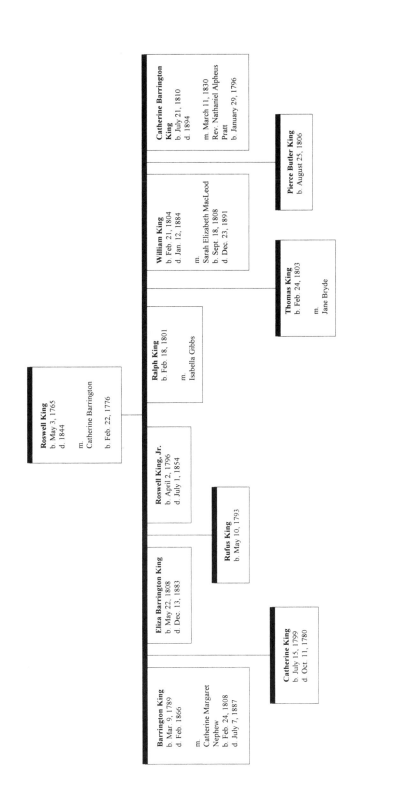

Roswell King
b. May 3, 1765
d. 1844

m.
Catherine Barrington
b. Feb. 22, 1776

Barrington King
b. Mar. 9, 1789
d. Feb. 1866

m.
Catherine Margaret
Nephew
b. Feb 24, 1808
d. July 7, 1887

Catherine King
b. July 15, 1799
d. Oct. 11, 1780

Eliza Barrington King
b. May 22, 1808
d. Dec. 13, 1883

Rufus King
b. May 10, 1793

Roswell King, Jr.
b. April 2, 1796
d. July 1, 1854

Ralph King
b. Feb. 18, 1801

m.
Isabella Gibbs

Thomas King
b. Feb. 24, 1803

m.
Jane Bryde

William King
b. Feb 21, 1804
d. Jan 12, 1884

m.
Sarah Elizabeth MacLeod
b. Sept. 18, 1808
d. Dec. 23, 1891

Pierce Butler King
b. August 25, 1806

Catherine Barrington King
b. July 21, 1810
d. 1894

m. March 11, 1830
Rev. Nathaniel Alpheus
Pratt
b. January 29, 1796

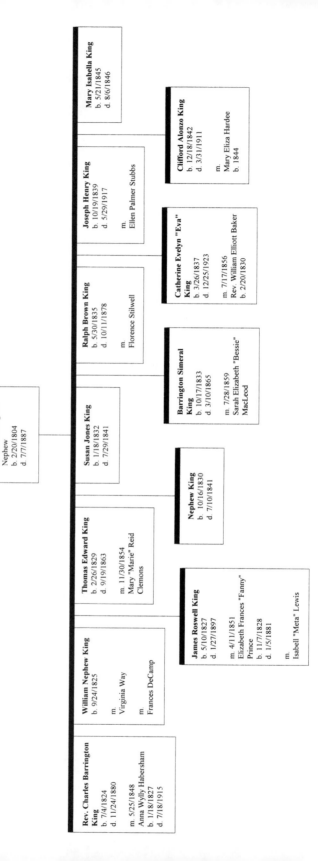

Barrington King
b. 3/9/1798
d. 2/1866

m. 1/30/1822
Catherine Margaret Nephew
b. 2/20/1804
d. 7/7/1887

Rev. Charles Barrington King
b. 7/4/1824
d. 11/24/1880

m 5/25/1848
Anna Wylly Habersham
b. 1/18/1827
d. 7/18/1915

William Nephew King
b. 9/24/1825

m.
Virginia Way

m.
Frances DeCamp

Thomas Edward King
b. 2/26/1829
d. 9/19/1863

m. 11/30/1854
Mary "Marie" Reid Clemons

James Roswell King
b. 5/10/1827
d. 1/27/1897

m. 4/11/1851
Elizabeth Frances "Fanny" Prince
b. 11/7/1828
d. 1/5/1881

m.
Isabell "Meta" Lewis

Nephew King
b. 10/16/1830
d. 7/10/1841

Susan Jones King
b. 1/18/1832
d. 7/29/1841

Barrington Simeral King
b. 10/17/1833
d. 3/10/1865

m. 7/28/1859
Sarah Elizabeth "Bessie" MacLeod

Ralph Brown King
b. 5/30/1835
d. 10/11/1878

m.
Florence Stilwell

Catherine Evelyn "Eva" King
b. 3/26/1837
d. 12/25/1923

m. 7/17/1856
Rev. William Elliott Baker
b. 2/20/1830

Joseph Henry King
b. 10/19/1839
d. 5/29/1917

m.
Ellen Palmer Stubbs

Clifford Alonzo King
b. 12/18/1842
d. 3/31/1911

m.
Mary Eliza Hardee
b. 1844

Mary Isabella King
b. 5/21/1845
d. 8/6/1846

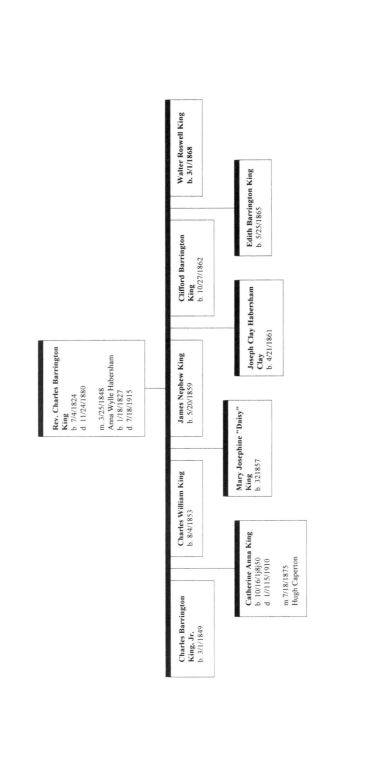

Rev. Charles Barrington King
b. 7/4/1824
d. 11/24/1880

m. 3/25/1848
Anna Wylle Habersham
b. 1/18/1827
d. 7/18/1915

Walter Roswell King
b. 3/1/1868

Clifford Barrington King
b. 10/27/1862

Edith Barrington King
b. 5/25/1865

James Nephew King
b. 5/20/1859

Joseph Clay Habersham Clay
b. 4/21/1861

Charles William King
b. 8/4/1853

Mary Josephine "Daisy" King
b. 321857

Charles Barrington King, Jr.
b. 3/1/1849

Catherine Anna King
b. 10/16/1j8J50
d. 1/115/1910

m. 7/18/1875
Hugh Caperton

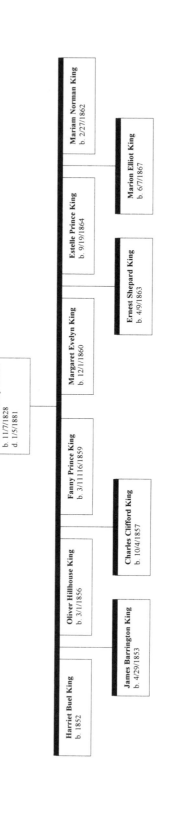

James Roswell King
b. 5/10/1827
d. 1/27/1897

m. 4/11/1851
Elizabeth Frances
Hillhouse "Franny" Prince
b. 11/7/1828
d. 1/5/1881

Harriet Buel King
b. 1852

James Barrington King
b. 4/29/1853

Oliver Hillhouse King
b. 3/1/1856

Charles Clifford King
b. 10/4/1857

Fanny Prince King
b. 3/11/1859

Margaret Evelyn King
b. 12/1/1860

Ernest Shepard King
b. 4/9/1863

Estelle Prince King
b. 9/19/1864

Mariam Norman King
b. 2/27/1862

Marion Elliot King
b. 6/7/1867

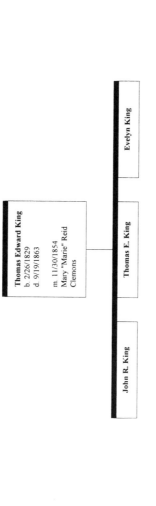

Thomas Edward King
b. 2/26/1829
d. 9/19/1863

m 11/30/1854
Mary "Marie" Reid
Clemons

John R. King

Thomas E. King

Evelyn King

Barrington Simeral King
b. 10/17/1833
d. 3/10/1865

m. July 28, 1859
Sarah Elizabeth "Bessie" MacLeod
b 8/27/1840

Harris MacLeod King
b. abt 1860

m.
Georgia "Georgie" Baker

Barrington "Bubba" King
b. 1862
d. 5/26/1884

Catherine Margaret "Maggie" King
b. 1864
d. 5/26/1866

INTRODUCTION

Roswell King established the community, or the Colony as it has been referred to repeatedly, of Roswell, Georgia, at a location he found during his travels into north Georgia in search of gold in 1828.[1] These lands had only recently been opened to white settlement following the removal of the Cherokee Indians. King, who lived in Darien (McIntosh County) since moving to Georgia at the age of twenty-three from Windsor, Connecticut, worked as a representative for the Bank of Darien. He was impressed with the possibility of mixing agriculture and industry in this community. The site offered a water force of Cedar (Vickery) Creek flowing into the Chattahoochee River, allowing him to build various water-powered mills not far from the fields that produced the raw materials. Prior to his job with the bank, King worked at many other jobs and played various roles in his community, including overseer of the estate of Pierce Butler on St. Simons Island until Roswell King, Jr., took over this task;[2] surveyor for Glynn County; justice of the peace and justice of the inferior court of Glynn and McIntosh counties; a lumber measurer; a member of the Georgia Militia; and a member of the Georgia House of Representatives in 1794–1795.[3] King was also credited with being the contractor of a twenty-room house of

[1] Sarah Joyce King Cooper, *King and Allied Families* (Athens GA: Agee Publishers, Inc., 1992) 36.

[2] Richard G. Coleman, *A Short History of the Roswell Manufacturing Company of Roswell, Georgia: Home of "Roswell Grey"* (N.p.: 1982) 2.

[3] Cooper, *King and Allied Families*, 26.

tabby, which was to be used as a hotel. Although the house appears not to have been successful as a hotel, Roswell King's family, along with the families of his brothers, Reuben and Thomas, resided there for a period of time.

Roswell, Georgia, was established in 1836,[4] when Roswell King was seventy years old. Roswell King and one of his sons, Barrington King, a director of the Bank of Darien,[5] led a group of six coastal families to settle the area, which became known as "the Colony."[6] The founding citizens of Roswell were a small, select group. Along with Roswell King were his widowed daughter, Eliza King Hand, and her children. Their neighbors were James Stephens Bulloch, John Dunwody, Reverend Nathaniel Alpheus Pratt,[7] and Archibald Smith and their families.

The homes built by each settler demonstrated his wealth. Roswell King first built a log cabin, the Castle, and then built Primrose Cottage. After his first cabin, which was a temporary location later used as a kitchen for his mansion, Barrington King built Barrington Hall, a Greek Revival mansion, completed in 1842. He employed builder/architect Willis Ball from Connecticut for its construction. Ball remained in Roswell two years after the completion of Barrington Hall.

The Bullochs built Bulloch Hall, completed in 1840. The Dunwodys built Dunwody Hall, which burned down during a

---

[4] Ibid., 37. Questionable date, other sources have 1832 as establishment date.

[5] Clarece Martin, *A History of Roswell Presbyterian Church* (Dallas: Taylor Publishing Company, 1984) 16.

[6] Arthur N. Skinner & James L. Skinner, eds., *The Death of a Confederate: Selections from the Letters of the Archibald Smith Family of Roswell, Georgia, 1864–1956* (Athens: University of Georgia Press, 1996) xvi.

[7] Reverend Nathaniel Alpheus Pratt married Catherine King, a daughter of Roswell King. The Pratts had seven sons.

housewarming party and was rebuilt and renamed Phoenix Hall.[8] Later the name was changed again, this time to Mimosa Hall. The Presbyterian minister, Reverend Nathaniel Alpheus Pratt, and his wife Catherine King, daughter of Roswell King, built Great Oaks, completed in 1842. North of the settlement, the Smiths built what in their family correspondence is described as a farmhouse.[9]

According to one secondary source, the Kings came to north Georgia from the coast with more than forty slaves.[10] Although the exact number of slaves is not proven, it obviously would have taken numerous hands to clear the land, construct the plantations, construct the mills, and build the dam that supplied energy to run the mills. The dam was 30 feet high and was built of mud, rocks, and logs cut in making the road down the slope of Vickery's Creek. Using the dam for waterpower, the Kings built a sawmill to cut lumber for the construction of the houses. In addition to a cotton mill and a sawmill, the Kings also built a brick kiln and made bricks for the many mills and houses they were constructing.[11]

The industrial part of this community was embodied by the Roswell Manufacturing Company founded in 1839 by Roswell King for the production of cotton goods. The Georgia General Assembly incorporated the Roswell Manufacturing Company on 11 December 1839. This first mill was built close to Vickery's Creek and was a large building for its time, rising four stories high and 88 feet long by 48 feet wide and constructed of brick.[12]

---

[8] Caroline Matheny Dillman, *Days Gone By in Alpharetta and Roswell Georgia* (Roswell GA: Chattahoochee Press, 1992).

[9] Skinner & Skinner, *Death of a Confederate,* xvi.

[10] Coleman, *A Short History,* 2.

[11] Ibid., 3.

[12] Ibid.

Following the death of Roswell King on 15 February 1844, the Roswell Manufacturing Company continued to grow under the direction of the new president, Roswell's son Barrington King. In addition to cotton goods, the mill was producing woolen goods by 1846. The factory was a thriving business by the late 1840s, operating 3,500 spindles and 40 looms with 150 employees. At top production, the factory used five bales of cotton a day.[13]

As the business expanded each year, the factory grew to accommodate the growth. By 1853 a second cotton mill was built, bringing the value of the company, which included a woolen mill and a flourmill, to $220,000.[14] Barrington King's two eldest sons, James Roswell King and Thomas Edward King, built a third dam to power a woolen mill called Ivy Mill.

Employees were needed in the operations of these factories. The colony founded by five coastal families grew as the number of jobs increased. On 16 February 1854 the Georgia General Assembly issued a charter incorporating the town of Roswell, Georgia.

Just prior to the Civil War, the Kings' mills were filling orders for yarn, cloth, and rope for customers in northern cities such as Baltimore, Philadelphia, and Newark. Meanwhile, contacts were being made with other cities in the South, increasing the demand of the products. The Kings began to diversify, making tenting, flannel, and a blend of cotton and wool known as Roswell Grey. This blend was warmer than flannel but would not shrink like wool. The natural fibers gave the cloth a light shade of grey. Roswell Grey would become the cloth chosen to make uniforms for Confederate officers.[15]

---

[13] Ibid., 4–5.

[14] $220,000 in 1853 would be worth $4,393,565.99 in 2000.

[15] Coleman, *A Short History,* 5.

In the years just before the war began, the Roswell Manufacturing Company consisted of six buildings including a dye building, a picker building, a tannery, and two warehouses. The main mill had grown from the original dimensions to be 140 feet long and 53 feet wide. A new dam was also built with a larger, overshoot waterwheel, measuring 16 by 20 feet, to power the facilities.[16]

When the war began, six of Barrington King's sons enlisted in the Confederate Army. Thomas Edward King, James Roswell King, Ralph Brown King, and Joseph Henry King served in the cavalry of the Roswell Battalion, Company A, with Thomas having earlier served in Company C of the same. Thomas and James obtained the rank of Captain while Ralph served in Company B as a senior first lieutenant and Joseph served as a first lieutenant. Barrington Simeral King enlisted in Cobb's Legion, first with Company C and later with Company E, obtaining the rank of lieutenant colonel at the death of Colonel W. G. Delony on 6 November 1863. Clifford Alonzo King, the youngest of the King sons, served as a cadet in Georgia's Infantry, 3rd Battalion.

Thomas Edward King was elected captain of Company H, 7th Regiment, Georgia Infantry, Confederate Army, on 31 May 1861 and was severely wounded in the leg at First Bull Run on 21 July 1861. After some time, Thomas rejoined the Confederate Army and had the role of captain in command of the Roswell Battalion, which he left on 12 September 1863[17] in order to

---

[16] Ibid.

[17] Upon approving his leaving, Col. M. H. Wright recommended that Thomas King "instruct the officer left in command of your company to be extremely cautious and vigilant." This included keeping "cavalry pickets and scouts well out in front" of Roswell and Atlanta with no movement going unnoticed (US War Department, comp., *The War of the Rebellion: A Compilation of the Official Records of the Union and Confederate Armies,* 128

participate at the Battle of Chickamauga, where he served as a captain in the Confederate Army. He was killed 19 September 1863 in that battle.

Cobb's Legion is perhaps one of the most infamous regiments of soldiers in the Civil War. Having joined Cobb's Legion in 1861, Barrington S. King went to Virginia to participate in the war as a part of the Cobb-Cobb-Wofford-DuBose Brigade of the Army of Northern Virginia. Under the leadership of Howell Cobb and his brother, Thomas Reade Rootes Cobb, the forces of Cobb's Legion, part mounted and part infantry, served the Confederacy far beyond the participation and the lives of the two brothers whose name it bore. Howell Cobb was promoted to brigadier general on 13 February 1862 and was detached and returned to Georgia October 1862. T. R. R. Cobb died from wounds suffered at the Battle of Fredericksburg in December 1862. Cobb's Legion participated in many of the great engagements of the Civil War including Yorktown, Lee's Mill, Seven Days battles, Fredericksburg, Gettysburg, Lee's Retreat from Gettysburg to Falling Waters, the Wilderness Campaign, where Barrington S. King was wounded in a charge, Spotsylvania Court House, Cold Harbor, New Market, Trevilian Station, Sharpsburg, Brandy Station, Carolina's Campaign, the Maryland Campaign, Second Manassas, the Knoxville Campaign, the Bristoe Campaign, and the Battle of Bentonville.

According to a Union report written March 1862, Cobb's Legion consisted of about 400 cavalry, armed with Maynard's rifles, and 600 infantry, all from Georgia.[18] The popularity of T. R. R. Cobb is demonstrated in the number of men willing to follow him into battle. In April of the same year, T. R. R. Cobb received a letter from Secretary of War George W. Randolph,

---

vols. [Washington, DC: 1880–1902] ser. 1, vol. 30, p. 643 [hereafter cited as *OR.*]).

[18] *OR,* ser. 1, vol. 11, pt. 1, p. 267.

granting the right to increased the legion's cavalry and infantry to eight companies. Cobb was given the choice either to increase in the legionary form or to increase each to a regiment, thereby dividing the legion. Beyond those already enlisted, the letter indicates that Cobb had additional men who would make up three more units. He was instructed by Randolph to tell those men in Georgia that they would not be joining Cobb's Legion due to the restraints of the legionary structure, and based on those restraints the Confederate military would no longer grant permission to form legions.[19]

In September 1864, two deserters from Cobb's Legion, natives of Maine who had lived in the South five years and had been conscripted just three months before, gave detailed accounts of the status of the Confederate military. These details were sent to the headquarters of the Army of the Potomac. From what the two deserters had witnessed and overheard, conclusions were drawn that Hampton's command could mount no more than 4,500 men and had 2,000 unmounted. In Cobb's Legion there were 100 mounted men and 400 unmounted. The 7th Georgia had about 40 mounted and 350 dismounted. Dearing's and Gary's brigades were nearly all mounted. These numbers demonstrate the shortage of horses the Confederate Army faced in fall 1864.[20]

Cobb's Legion continued to fight until they surrendered at Appomattox Courthouse 26 April 1865. The interest in this legion and it soldiers has often surprised many historians. Perhaps the popularity of the young T. R. R. Cobb who died in battle added interest and loyalty to the legion. Others point to the interest in the legion due to its having been immortalized in Margaret Mitchell's *Gone with the Wind* as the legion the young Ashley Wilkes joins. In any case, the legend of Cobb's Legion

---

[19] *OR,* ser. 4, vol. 1, pt. 1, p. 1052.
[20] *OR,* ser. 1, vol. 42, pt. 2, pp. 688, 698.

has remained an intricate part of the Civil War for Southerners, particularly Georgians.

During the war, the Roswell Manufacturing Company supported the cause by donating cotton sheeting to many hospitals and selling material to the state. As the Union army approached Roswell, many citizens felt it was wise to move their families. Barrington King moved his family to Savannah and was rumored to have moved his household items to a house he had bought in Atlanta.[21]

Confederate forces in Roswell were under the command of Captain James R. King, one of Barrington's sons. As General Joseph E. Johnston fell back across the Chattahoochee River, the Roswell Battalion fell back as well, burning the bridge crossing the river and leaving Roswell, on the north banks of the Chattahoochee River, open to the Union cavalry.

The Union cavalry, under the leadership of Brigadier General Kenner Garrard, destroyed the Roswell Manufacturing Company's mills with direct orders from General William T. Sherman early in July 1864. They burned all but the Ivy Mill, which was under the management of a French national, Theophile Roche. The Ivy Mill had been turned over to Roche by the Kings in hopes it would be spared. However, the flying of the French flag was not able to save the mill. When Roche was unable to produce a United States flag to fly above the mill, the machinery of the Ivy Mill was thrown into the river and a small fire was started in the mill, damaging but not completely destroying it. Days later, the remaining boards were used by General Greenville M. Dodge to build a 600-foot bridge over the Chattahoochee River.

Brigadier General Garrard had been instructed by General William T. Sherman to arrest the owners and all those employed in the mills for treason, which allegedly totaled about 400

---

[21] Coleman, *A Short History,* 6.

women.[22] These women were marched to Marietta, imprisoned in the Georgia Military Institute, and placed on a train headed north to Nashville on 15 July. They were sent from Nashville to Louisville on 21 July, and then across the river to Jeffersonville, Indiana, where they were set free.[23] This particular incident caused much outrage as it ran in Northern newspapers. Many of these women were sent away with no method of letting their husbands, many of whom were Confederate soldiers, or their families know of their location. Personal stories of what happened to these women have been reported on numerous occasions. General Sherman chose not to mention this incident in his official memoirs.

Most of the mill owners had fled Roswell when the Confederate forces retreated just days before Roswell was occupied by Garrard and his men. Barrington King and his wife went to Savannah during summer 1864 and returned to Roswell in June 1865, after the war had ended, to survey the damage. Among those who remained in Roswell throughout the war were Reverent Pratt, who is credited with saving the church's silver communion service.

In their own words, the family members indicate a devotion to each other and to their fair Roswell. By reading the actual letters, the reader is transported back in time, anticipating each letter with hope of good news from home or for good news from the front. Through these letters, the Civil Wars unfolds only as it can through primary documents. And as the family's experiences changed their lives forever, we share those changes and those feelings of uncertainty.

The correspondence begins at the coming of age of Barrington Simeral King, the seventh of Barrington King's twelve children, in 1858. The correspondence transcribed here

---

[22] Ibid., 7.

[23] Ibid.

focus on Barrington Simeral King, his father and mother, his wife, and other immediate family members, as well as his finances and interest in the Roswell Manufacturing Company. The earliest documents are shares in the Roswell Manufacturing Company being bought by William H. McLeod, future father-in-law of Barrington S. King. Now, in their own words, is the Civil War experience of the King family of Roswell, Georgia.

CORRESPONDENCE

As this book begins, the main character, Barrington S. King, goes from being a bachelor to a devoted husband concerned about the well-being of his family. The earliest correspondence is of stocks held in the Roswell Manufacturing Company and issued by his father, Barrington King.

Georgia $2300

Cobb Co

This will certify that Wm H. McLeod[1] Esq [Esquire] is the proprietor of Two shares of the capital stock Roswell Manfg Co of Cobb county, on which Eleven hundred & fifty dollars for share have been paid.

Roswell 31 March 1858

B. King

H.W. Proudfoot[2]

Book Keeper   Ros: Manf g Co

---

[1] William Harris MacLeod was the father of Barrington Simeral King's future bride, Sarah Elizabeth "Bessie" MacLeod. Bessie's mother was Martha Salmon.

[2] H. W. Proudfoot lived next door to the Kings according to the 1860 census, which listed his employment as a bookkeeper. The census listed his real estate property value to be $1500, and his personal estate was worth $500 (US Bureau of the Census, *1860 Census of Population* [Washington, DC: Government Printing Office]).

Georgia $5750
Cobb Co

This will certify that Richd McLeod[3] Trustee for Miss Sarah
E. McLeod[4] is the proprietor of Five shares of the Capital Stock
Roswell Manfg Co Cobb county, on which Eleven hundred &
fifty dollars for share have been paid. Roswell 31 March 1858

                                         B. King

H.W. Proudfoot
     Book Keeper   Ros: Manf g Co

                                 Roswell August 28 1858

My Dearest Mother

Your sweet letter was received by wednesdays mail. It made
me happy indeed that Father and yourself were so well pleased
with my engagement to Bessie MacLeod[5] and seemed willing that
I should marry her next spring, although having no means of
support other than your help. Since writing my last to you, B-
[Bessie] thinks we will have to wait until the latter part of may,
or first of June when her relations will have come up to spend the
summer,[6] and can be present on the occasion. As much as I hate
to defer it so long, dear Mother, I know it will be best, as it will
give me three months practice where I am going to settle, which
will be of great advantage to all parties. I wont decide much on
anything though before having a talk with Father and yourself in
Atlanta on my way north.

---

[3] Richard Habersham MacLeod was Bessie's uncle.

[4] Sarah Elizabeth "Bessie" MacLeod, Barrington S. King's future wife.

[5] The spelling of this name is inconsistent in primary sources. Original
spelling is retained in letters and quotations; otherwise, "MacLeod" is used.

[6] From their home on the coast, probably Savannah.

Mother, my dearest mother, I have seen the wickedness of my heart, and I hope God has through his Son cleansed it, and given me a clean heart. And with his strong arm to help me, I feel that I can now lead the life of a christian. I have had several conversations with Uncle.[7] What first made me see my own sinfulness, was Bs- pure womanly love, when I determined to live a new life. For some weeks I lived on in a cloak of self righteousness, But I soon saw without Gods help I could do nothing. And I prayed earnestly for weeks that God would take away my self righteousness, and humble me to the dust at the foot of the cross of Jesus Christ. Since last Tuesday I have felt my burden lighter, and my love to God greater. Oh! Mother pray that my conversion may be sincere, and that God will give me much grace to fight against the wills and the temptations of the evil one—I asked Uncle to bring forward the communion sabbath to the last Sunday in September, so as to allow me to unite with the [First Presbyterian] church in Roswell before I left home, as it may be the last communion sabbath I ever may be at in Roswell. And I would rather leave home after making a public profession of religion as it must certainly would strengthen me in right ways. I wish I could see you now to converse with you, dearest mother—

I hope you are having a pleasant time away from home and enjoying yourself much. We are getting along very well at home. I had a little *flare up* with Sister Anna[8] some time since about the noise the children make at table, and now they eat in the pantry,

---

[7] Rev. Nathaniel Pratt, husband of Barrington's father's youngest sister, was the pastor of the First Presbyterian Church of Roswell. Perhaps one of the most noteworthy services he performed was the marriage of Martha "Mittie" Bulloch and Theodore Roosevelt, Sr.

[8] Anna Wylly Habersham, wife of Barrington's oldest brother, Rev. Charles Barrington King. The noisy children would have been his nephews and nieces: Catherine Anna King, age eight; Habersham King, age six; Charles William King, age five; and Mary Josephine "Daisy" King, age one year.

which is much pleasant for us, and they seem happier— Dr Habersham and wife[9] are with us this week, they leave Monday next for Savannah. Bro Charles[10] has come up for the rest of the summer. All are pretty well and send much love— Mr Adams[11] is getting along very well and I expect when you see him north next month can congratulate him as he is going to propose the day before he goes north. Give my love to Uncle Styles family and Coz Sue.[12] Keep much for Father and yourself.

Your Affectionate Son,
B S King

Bessie got her wish, and the wedding was held off until the following summer when she and Barrington Simeral King married on 28 July 1859.

In the 1859 Atlanta city directory, Barrington S. King is listed as a Homeopathic Physician with his office on Peachtree Street between Decatur and Houston streets on Cherokee Block. He was boarding at John Glenn's. King had paid extra to have his name in a larger print.[13]

---

[9] Joseph Clay Habersham, M.D., and his wife, Ann Wylly Adams, were the parents of Anna Wylly Habersham.

[10] Barrington's eldest brother, Rev. Charles Barrington King.

[11] Probably a brother of Anna Wylly Adams.

[12] Joseph Clay Styles (sometimes spelled "Stiles") was married to Caroline Clifford Nephew, the half sister of Barrington S. King's mother. Cousin Sue was Sue Thirston.

[13] *Williams' Atlanta City Directory for 1859–1860* (Atlanta: M. Lynch, 1859).

Another year passes before additional information about
Barrington S. King is found. He has moved Bessie to Columbia,
South Carolina, and is attempting to establish himself as a
homeopathic physician there. The following letter lends insight
into King's lifestyle growing up, a lifestyle he now could not
afford.

Columbia   August 10th 1860

My Dear Father

I wrote you two days ago, telling you of an opportunity I
had of taking the house & office now occupied by Pfonts,[14] and
asking your opinion & advice. I have not been able to wait for
either, as Pfonts having an offer to be bought out, told me he
would give me the preference, but would like for me to decide
immediately. I have therefore decided upon taking it, & making
the most of my opportunity. I am certain I could not do better
or as well if I waited years. I also had a talk with the owner Dr.
Geiger[15] a man of some prominence, and whose word can be
relied on perhaps as well as any bodys so I am told. He told me I
could take the house as soon as Pfonts was ready to let me have
it. That I could keep it as long as I wanted it, rent $2.50—pr
year for house & office payable quarterly. That I could leave it at
the end of any quarter & that in case he had to sell or should
want it he would give me 6 months notice. All very fair for me.
The House has 4 rooms in it. Parlor 15 x 15, dining room 10 1/2
x 11 1/2, bed room 12 x 15, bed room 10 1/2 x 11 1/2. very
unpretending as you see, but large enough for us to be perfectly
comfortable. In the yard is a kitchen with *svts* [servant's] room;

---

[14] Mr. Pfonts occupied the property, house, and office.

[15] Charles A. Geiger.

a store room; & quite a nice stable & carriage house. So I can keep my horse at less than 1/2 what it costs at the stable.

The house looks very neat on the outside, with good fence around it. I dont think any of our acquaintances will cat us, as it is more the *persons* than the *show* they make that makes society in this place, & one of the deacons of our church lives in a house exactly like ours only not quite so neat externally. As far as location is concerned, it is the choicest one of all for an M.D. I told you the articles that I would want of Pfonts amounted to $110. Since then I have concluded to take one of his bedsteads with spring mattress which I got for $20- (cost $35 last fall and perfectly good now) & his office furniture $15- making in all $145-. There are a number of little articles indispensable in housekeeping all of which are perfectly good & by comparing prices at Store I find I get them at from 25 to 40 prct [percent] less than they cost. But now Father for what is troubling me. To pay expenses & commence housekeeping I will require $223- besides the $100 I wrote for last week, viz:

To pay Pfonts for articles bought . . .	*$145.00*
Rent of Present office to 1st Sept . . .	$ 17.00
Our board to 21st August . . .	$ 75.00
Horse do " do...[ditto]	$ 22.00
For medicines I have sent for	$ 14.00
To buy sheets & c. [etc.] also for provisions for Sept	$ 50.00
Total	$323.00
Less $100- which I have written for	*$100__*
	$223.00

There is not that amount to my credit But Father if you can only advance for me until the next dividends,[16] which although they may not be as much as usual, I assure you we can live so much cheaper keeping house that I will be able to get along. The medicines sent for were some absolutely required. I am determined to live economically, and deny myself every thing that is not absolutely necessary. I would not move into the house before 1st of Sept, but as I have to pay rent from the 15th inst,[17] & it will also save $25 by moving in on the 21st, I have concluded to go into it on that day.

Please Father help us by advancing what we may need, and give us a start, after which I am confidant we can save something. Your letter was recd [received] this morning and I thank you again for the servants[18] you will give us. Could you please send them to us letting them leave Roswell in the waggons on Monday the 20th so that they will get here on the 21st? And I will be at the depôt to receive them when the cars arrive. If you can spare Harriet[19] to us until the 1st of Sept. when we will be pretty well under way, I will send her leaving here on the 3rd of Sept. and she will get there the next day.

Just let us get once fairly started Father and I am determined to live at less expense than we have been at heretofore. It can be done and it shall be done.

Am sorry to hear Old John[20] is so sick. Its the first I have heard of it, but hope he may recover. The crops have improved

---

[16] Dividends from the family business, the Roswell Manufacturing Company.

[17] Abbreviation for instant, which means of the current month (*Webster's New Twentieth Century Dictionary of the English Language*, unabridged, 2d ed. [New York: The World Publishing Company, 1971]).

[18] The Kings referred to their slaves as servants.

[19] A female slave belonging to Barrington King.

[20] A male slave belonging to Barrington King.

considerably in this section since the rain, & hope yours will turn out better than you expect.

Bessie joins with me in much love to yourself & dear Mother. If you can send the amnt [amount] required please Father send it on receipt of this & oblige Your Affectionate Son

B.S. King

B. S. King joined Cobb's Legion, which was organized by Howell Cobb during spring 1861 in Georgia, consisting of cavalry, infantry, and artillery but not serving as one command. The artillery company acted independently and was known as the Troup Light Artillery. Soon after its formation the unit was moved to Virginia.

The cavalry battalion consisted of men from Richmond, Fulton, and Dougherty counties, Georgia, and contained six companies. With the addition of five more companies, there were a total of eleven companies until July 1864. It was at this time that one company, totaling 526 officers and men, was transferred to Phillips' Georgia Legion.

The cavalry's official title was the 9th Georgia Cavalry, but this term is rarely used. The unit served in Major General Wade Hampton's division in P. M. B. Young's[21] Brigade under Colonel

---

[21] Pierce Manning Butler Young, CSA general, had attended the Georgia Military Academy and West Point, where he would have graduated with the class of 1861 if he had not left to side with his state, South Carolina. He served as adjutant in Cobb's Legion early in the war, was made lieutenant colonel and commanded the legion at South Mountain and Fredericksburg, was promoted to colonel before Brandy Station, and fought at Gettysburg before being named brigadier general on 28 September 1863. In December 1864 he was promoted to major general (Mark Mayo Boatner III, *The Civil War Dictionary,* rev. ed. [New York: David McKay Company, Inc.] 953).

J. Frederick Waring.[22] The unit participated in numerous conflicts including the Seven Days battles, Cold Harbor, Brandy Station, Gettysburg, and later numerous engagements south and north of the James River. In 1865 the command was attached to T. M. Logan's Brigade. They fought in the Carolinas and were present at the surrender of the Army of Tennessee.

The command suffered heavy losses, demonstrated by 3 officers and 41 men at Brandy Station and 21 casualties of the 330 engaged at Gettysburg.

The field officers were Colonel Pierce M. B. Young and Colonel Gilbert J. Wright. Lieutenant colonels were W. G. Delony and Barrington S. King. Majors were Z. A. Rice and Benjamin C. Yancey.[23]

From early August through early September, Cobb's Legion, Cavalry Battalion, remained at Camp Cobb in Henrico County, Virginia, located 1 mile from the State House in Richmond on the racetrack of the old Richmond fairgrounds. From 1 September 1861 through 10 October 1861, Cobb's Legion, both the infantry and cavalry, camped at Camp Washington in York County, Virginia, located 2 miles southeast of Yorktown.

During mid-October, the troops stayed in a temporary camp called Camp Mud Hole while the men were building huts for winter quarters at Camp Marion. During December of the first year, the legion spent some time in Camp Disappointment in York County, Virginia, which was a picket camp located on the peninsula below Camp Marion. The main camp for the legion that winter was Camp Marion in York County, Virginia, from mid-October until early January and from mid-January to early March. Camp Marion was located 7 miles below Yorktown.

---

[22] *OR*, ser. 1, vol. 42, pt. 3, p. 1243.

[23] Joseph H. Crute, Jr., *Units of the Confederate States Army* (Midlothian VA: Derwent Books, 1987) 118.

In March 1862 the legion was at Camp Hunter in Suffolk County, Virginia, located a little over a mile from the center of Suffolk on the Norfolk and Petersburg Railroad. From mid-March to the first week of April, the troops camped at Camp Randolph in Wayne County, North Carolina, located in a pine grove beside the railroad, 4 miles below Goldsboro. Cobb's Legion appeared at Camp Caroline, Spotsylvania County, Virginia, between the Rappahannock River and the headwaters of the Mattaponi on 16 May 1862.

Later in May the legion was stationed at Camp Winder in Henrico County, Virginia, which was located near the Richmond reservoir and Hollywood Cemetery, about 1 mile northwest of Richmond. In early June the troops were located at Camp Young, Henrico County, Virginia, which was in an oak grove about 2.5 miles from Richmond and about 2.5 miles from the enemy's pickets.[24]

The following appraisal document was for Company E of Cobb's Legion. Two copies of this appraisal exist in the King family papers.

Appraisement of Horses & Horse Equipments of members of Capt B S Kings Cavalry Company Cobbs Georgia Legion who were absent at first Appraisement

Valuation in Dollars

---

[24] William S. Smedlund, *Camp Fires of Georgia's Troops, 1861–1865* (Lithonia GA: Kennesaw Mountain Press, 1994) 284–85, 83, 217, 113, 198, 160, 234, 92–93, 293, 298.

Rank		Horses	Equipments
3rd Lieut	Leonzo D Johnson[25]	225.	45.
1st Corp	John N Brooks		10.Saddle
Private	Allbritten John A	175.	
Do [Ditto]	Allbritten William A		25.Saddle
Do	Chambers James B	200.	
Do	Mills James W	185.	35.Saddle
Do	Murdock Charles A	183.	
Do	Owens John W	185.	
Do	Ramsey S. Thomas	~~250.~~	
Do	South Amaziah[26]	190.	
		(over)	

We certify, on oath that the figures opposite the names on this Roll, for valuation of horses & horse equipments, represent & show the true cash value of the horse & equipments of the men, respectively, at the place of enrollment according to our honest, impartial judgement.

Wm M Williams
Capt
E J Appling   Appraisers
T.H. Williams
Sworn to & subscribed before
Date: June 6th 1862
Station: Camp Meadows[27] near Richmond

---

[25] Leonidas D. Johnson was listed as a first lieutenant in Cobb's Legion.

[26] Amaziah South obtained the rank of sergeant by the end of the war.

[27]Camp Meadow was located in Henrico County VA about 3 miles north of Richmond. Cobb's Legion, Cavalry Battalion, was known to have been stationed there from 8–25 June 1862, 5–7 July 1862, and 20–21 July 1862 (Smedlund, *Camp Fires,* 207).

❖

From 25 June through 1 July 1862, Cobb's Legion, as part of the Army of Northern Virginia under General Robert E. Lee and as part of Mayor General J. B. Magruder's Division/Second Brigade with Brigade General Howell Cobb in command of the Brigade, participated in the Seven Days battles. In that battle, the Brigade had 66 soldiers killed, 347 wounded, and 2 missing in action at the end of the battle.

On 4 July 1862 Cobb's Legion, Cavalry Battalion, was camped at Camp Battalion in Henrico County, Virginia, located 3 miles north oF Richmond. During the months of October and December, the legion was stationed at Camp Rapidan in Orange County, Virginia, near Raccoon Ford on the Rapidan River. [28]

During this time King was working with the cavalry outpost and assisted Colonel James D. Nance of the 3rd South Carolina Regiment in collecting arms scattered about the battlefield. Arms collected that day by Nance, King, and Major White of the 7th South Carolina Regiment were 925. [29]

Although up to this point there have been few letters, we do find that by December Barrington and Bessie have two children, and Barrington has come home for a visit.

Marietta Dec 5th 1862

My Dear Father

Owing to delays in getting my boxes off I will not be able to leave myself before tomorrow. I neglected to tell you about one account I handed in. "J. M. Evans" I have forgotten the amnt [amount] I had due him, but whatever it is, please cross it & his name from the list, as he will be paid in Richmond when he

---

[28] Smedlund, *Camp Fires,* 61, 235.
[29] *OR,* ser. 1, vol. 11, pt. 2, p. 739.

comes on. Bessie & children quite well, & join with me in love to dear Mother, yourself & all. Mr. MacLeod[30] was too unwell to get up this morning.

Your Affectionate Son
B.S. King

The following letter from Barrington S. King to his father not only gives insight into the camp life of soldiers but also indicates the fighting taking place in Tennessee in December 1862 and January 1863.

❖

Camp near Raccoon Ford Rapidan River[31]
Jan 6th 1863

My Dear Father

I gave Bessie an account of the only scout our Regiment has been on since my return to camp, going out on Christmass day & returning on the 1st of January. And although a plenty affair and excitement, enough to make light the fatiques & hunger experienced on all such service, yet *what* a *contrast* to previous Christmass hollidays. Instead of the singing of bells; the clattering of the horses hoof. In place of the harmless reports of fire arms; the booming of cannon, the shricking of shell, the whistling of bullets bearing death on their course were heard. And instead of the joyous shouts of assemblies; the fierce yells of our

---

[30] William H. MacLeod was Bessie's father.

[31] Camp Rapidan was in Orange County VA near Raccoon Ford. Cobb's Legion, Cavalry Battalion, camped here during October and December 1862, according to Smedlund (*Camp Fires,* 235).

boys charging into the enemies ranks with uplighted sabres and cries of the wounded were the sounds to be heard. And last, but not least, in place of the plentiful and luxurious dinner of dear old home with the dear ones sitting around; crunched near a smokey fire, eating hungrily a piece of fat bacon broiled on coals with navy biscuit for bread, were all that we had for the days of the Christmass hollidays. But for all this the Regiment is in better health than ever before known, nearly every man in it weighing more than ever in their lives before. I have fattened so much that I can not button my coat or jacket and my sabre belt is two holes larger than I have ever known it. But oh! for an *honorable peace* to our unhappy country that we might all return to our homes and loved ones. We have heard the news of a great fight in Tennessee in which we were again victorious. *When will* our enemies become convinced of the *impossibility* of conquering us (*God being with us*) and give us the peace which we ask as our rights?

Since my return to camp my company has drawn pay for 6 months (up to Jan 1st), I enclose you a list of notes and amounts to be credited thereso, also notes & accounts of persons in Gwinnett Co. and account of persons living near Roswell. I have at Kent Paine and Co. $4200. After paying for the cook and some other things in Richmond the balance will be sent to you and if you would take the trouble to attend to these settlement you would oblige me very much. Opposite the names of some you will notice a X. "S.T. Ramsey[32] note to Arnold."[33] Ramsey wants the money kept by you till some understanding with Arnold the horse being sick when traded for. "Jas A. Voss[34] note

---

[32] S. Thomas Ramsey of Georgia served in Cobb's Legion, Company E.

[33] Probably Givins W. Arnold of Georgia, Cobb's Legion, Company E, senior 2d lieutenant.

[34] James A. Voss of Georgia served in Cobb's Legion, Company E.

to Webb[35]" and "A C Dickerson[36] note to Hook[37]" dont know whether their notes were with or without int. [interest]. If the parties insist on getting int. please pay it taking up the notes and let me know the amount. "B. Woodruff[38] note to McMullen[39]" Woodruff is dead. I have sold his horse and sent it with wages to his wife. There is only a small amnt to take up note ask her if she will pay it from the amount set to her. "Ira W. Owens[40] note to Bellah[41]" the horse was blind in one eye when sold to Owens. Bellah promised to deduct some. Owens paid $50 boot to get another horse. Bellah ought to ~~pay~~ deduct $25 from his note. The Gwinnett crowd I will write to and make time call on you for their moneys. "J.H. Bones[42] note to W.S. Walker"[43] make Walker show a showing from Bone for the amnt $103- or only pay him half of it. Bone was discharged & sold his horse. Cooleys[44] horse has only drawn pay for two month and a half $31-. It had better be placed on my note. In looking over the pay rolls I see $17.60 more due him in July, $8.80 for self same for horse. Give love to dear Mother. I am sorry she has been suffering as much with headache. Love to all at home I write to Bessie by the same mail.

Your Aft. [affectionate] Son,
B.S. King

---

[35] Bryce Webb of Georgia served in Cobb's Legion, Company C.

[36] Augustus C. Dickerson of Georgia served in Cobb's Legion, Company E.

[37] Lewis H. Hook of Georgia served in the Cherokee Legion, Company D.

[38] Berrimon Woodruff served in Cobb's Legion, Company E.

[39] Samuel P. McMullen served in the Cherokee Legion, Company D.

[40] Ira W. Owens served in Cobb's Legion, Company E.

[41] William P. Bellah served in Cobb's Legion, Company C.

[42] Joseph H. Bone served in Cobb's Legion, Company E.

[43] Not identifiable; someone who missed military duty.

[44] John Cooley served in Cobb's Legion, Company E.

P.S. I have deducted the balance S. P. McMullen note from Woodruff horse sale so please just pay it and say nothing to Mrs. Woodruff about it.

Your Son,
B.S. King

The letter Barrington wrote to Bessie the same day did not survive. Cobb's Legion was stationed at Camp Georgia in Culpeper County, Virginia, located 7 miles from Culpeper Court House during the middle to later part of January. From there they moved to Camp Stevensburg also in Culpeper County, Virginia, near Stevensburg, remaining there until mid-February. During February 1863, the infantry and cavalry of Cobb's Legion were permanently separated.[45]

The following is a letter to Bessie from Marie (Mary Reid Clemons), wife of Barrington's brother, Thomas Edward King. In the letter Marie writes of watching her husband suffer, and she writes about Edward being disappointed that he could not take part in the war. He had been elected Captain of Company H, 7th Regiment, Georgia Infantry, Confederate Army, on 31 May 1861, was severely wounded in the leg at First Bull Run on 21 July 1861, and was unable to resume command. It also gives the first indication of the traveling done by Bessie between Georgia and Virginia during the war.

---

[45] Smedlund, *Camp Fires,* 137, 61.

Roswell Feb 28th 1863.

My darling *Sister*

You have been in my thoughts, constantly, ever since I heard of your bitter disappointment & as I learn that you will not return immediately I thought I would write this morning to express my heartfelt sympathy, and to tell you how *very very* sorry I have felt for you in this great trial. I know *well* just how you must feel—but it is our Heavenly Father's will to lay this burden upon you, & as a Christian, I know you will try to be submissive.

Although it has pleased Him to lay upon you this particular cross, yet there are some [illegible]— your dear husband writes that he was never in more perfect health which must be a great comfort to you when so many return worn out, by wasting disease [dysentery], if not wounded & mained for life— How true it is that "every heart ruin with its own bitterness"— I have not had the auguish of a long continued separation from my beloved husband—but I have watched by his bedside in nights & days of pain, & heard gracious drown from him by acute agony—when it seemed as if every one would break my heart, have ever despaired of his life—& have yet been compelled to seem composed & cheerful.— This, thank God—is over—but still, I see Edward day after day, inwardly chafing that he is not persisted to take an active part in our struggle for independence- & still, in frequent pain—(for as he himself confesses, he *never* takes a step without pain) and with the prospect of being lame for life.— So, is it not true, dear Bessie, that we all have our peculiar troubles?— It may seem to you that there is nothing so bad as separation from your husband—but take heart of grace— reflect how many thousands there are in your situation—& would you have it *otherwise? You know* you would not, *brave* little patient as you are!— And when the war is over & Barringtons restored to your arms, as I believe & trust he will be—how *proud* you will be of him, and what a glorious thing to tell your boys, that their father fought through the war for freedom, & did *all* that *one arm might* for the establishment of our independence!———

These thoughts may be *some* comfort to you, dear Bessie, but still your heart must be *very sore*, & I pray that our Heavenly Father may strengthen & support you.

Edward has expressed his sorrow for your disappointment many times—every body seems to feel so much for you. Give my love to Cousin Jule,[46] Anna,[47] & all the family. Kiss the dear little boys for me & believe me ever

Your loving
Marie

Summer 1863 was a period of devastating battles including Gettysburg and Vicksburg. Because of these battles, many historians have classified that summer as the most crucial turning point in the American Civil War. The following gives an interesting account of battle.

Williamsport [Virginia] July 10*th* 1863

My own *precious darling*

A long long time has passed since I wrote you. I know you have been very uneasy about me. this is the first opportunity I have had of either writing or sending a letter since the last time I

---

[46] Julia Isabella Hand, daughter of Eliza Barrington King and Bayard Epenetus Hand and wife of Henry Montimer Anderson, was the niece of Barrington King.

[47] Anna Wylly Habersham, wife of Rev. Charles Barrington King, the eldest son of Barrington King and Catherine Margaret Nephew.

wrote after the Battle of Upperville.[48] Our campaign has been a terrible one. I cant enter into particulars but can thank God that my life & limb has been spared thus far & through two more severe fights. In a charge a week ago near Gettysburg in which Col. Delany[49] was wounded with a sabre cut over the head my horse ran away with me carrying me through almost the entire column of the enemy when running against the fence he fell throwing me heels over head I was considerably bruised but the fall saved my life. My horse jumped up & joined the Yankees with all my arms & accountisements & my saddle bags with many little valuables in them my needle book with my sleeve buttons in it all my hdks [handkerchiefs] & towels soap brush & comb & c. [etc.]. A serious loss to me but thank God my life was saved. We lost five Lts killed and five privates, one of my Lts among the number. I will give you all the particulars when we meet. I have been feeling badly ever since my fall & yesterday I had to succumb completely worn out with considerable fever. I feel better to day & am going across the river to a private house & remain in quiet for at least a week. I have much to tell you dearest of the incidents of our transpotomac campaign & the many narrow escapes God has blessed me with but I cant write them now. I have thought much & often of what your sufferings of mind are my precious one in not hearing from me & imagining the worst I am in hopes you are in Staunton[50] & have

---

[48] The Battle of Upperville took place in Upperville VA on 21 June 1863 and was part of the Gettysburg Campaign. This battle followed the battles of Aldie and Middleburg as Federal forces pressured the brigades of Hampton and Robertson to withdraw to Upperville. Wade Hampton led a series of charges against Gregg's division and relieved the pressure from the other brigades (Boatner, *Civil War Dictionary,* 861).

[49] William G. Delony, Cobb's Legion, Company C.

[50] Staunton VA is located west of the Blue Ridge Mountains.

enclosed this in one to Eva[51] who will forward [sic] it if you are not there. Oh if I could but have your sweet petting for a few days how sweet it would be. But dont feel uneasy about me, if I dont improve rapidly I will go to Staunton I would tell you to come to me if there was any danger of my being seriously ill But there is none at present. If you are still in Roswell you had better come on to Staunton at the first opportunity: But if you are in Staunton remain there until you hear further from me. Dont be uneasy about me for if I dont improve rapidly I will go to Staunton. I hope you are much better my darling my heart longs to see you that I may talk to you of all that is therein. Kiss my little darlings. give much love to all at home, Dear Mother, Father & all. May God bless you & permit us to meet in safety when this war ends ever prays your own much loving husband

B.S. King

In Colonel P. M. B. Young's report on the engagement of 9 July 1863, Brandy Station, he stated that King deserved "praise for the manner in which he commanded his sharpshooter."[52]

At this time, Cobb's Legion would have been stationed again at Camp Stevensburg in Culpeper County, Virginia, moving there the middle of August and remaining until the end of the month.[53]

The following letter expresses the South's need and desire for foreign intervention and also demonstrates the lack of value held in Confederate currency. By the time this letter was written, the eldest child of Barrington and Bessie, Harris, was left in

---

[51] Catherine Evelyn "Eva" King Baker was the sister of Barrington S. King.

[52] *OR,* ser. 1, vol. 27, pt. 2, p. 732.

[53] Smedlund, *Camp Fires,* 261.

Roswell with his grandparents while his mother went closer to the front.

Staunton August 21 1863

My Dear Father

I left Bessie at the Baths[54] yesterday on my way to the army. I had got well again, but was last night attacked with Dysenterry, I am better but will stay here until Monday when I hope to be perfectly well. I send my horses tomorrow & as it will be three days before they get to the Regt [regiment], it would be needless for me to get there before Monday evening. Your letter of the 13th was handed me here am glad to know there is a balance due me of $3200—. With the exception of a hundred or so to buy leather with, if you think it advisable I would like to have the remainder invested in cotton which is now worth about 50 cts per lb [cents per pound] in England & which when the war ends I can sell for specie at at least what its cost now is. & $3000 dollars in specie will be worth when the war *ends* more than ten times the amnt of C.S. [Confederate States] money. In fact I have no desire to hold an hundred dollars of money now issued by our government and hope you will use your own discretion & invest for me in anything you see fit. It will be impossible for me to think of money matters now or until the war ends, so I leave everything with you, Father, knowing that you will do for me the best you can. I also give you my power of Attorney to do and to act for me in my partnership with C.A. Geiger[55] in Card Clothing manufacture and am willing to abide by anything you may do or agree upon just as if I myself had done it. I hope though it will not or rather that you will not allow it to give you any trouble of

---

[54] The Alum Bath Springs in Bath County VA are thermal waters.

[55] Charles A. Geiger of Cobb County (*1860 Census of Population*).

body or of mind. I have very serious doubts of the machines[56] ever coming. If they come its a good investment if they fail to come the whole is money lost. I should hate much to lose what I invested, but do not yet regret that I did invest the money as I did I have written Dr Geiger telling him reasons why I would prefer having the machines opperated in Roswell. When I return to the Regt will write you again concerning notes & a/c [accounts] of men left with you. When you send lists of notes [I] will deduct for amount loaned in purchase of horses. You had better send them on as soon as possible as the men will draw in a few days.

Bessie has improved considerably But she is not well yet. Next week she is going to the Alum Springs. Eva[57] & children are going also, I have pursuaded her to do so. Baby[58] is improving very much. It was hard indeed to leave my wife but I have got well enough to help in the battles of our country & must go at her call. We are going to have some desperate fighting up here yet before this campaign ends but it is the last campaign of the war. We may lose Charleston, Savh [Savannah, Georgia] & Mobile [Alabama] yet before winter, that will only hasten foreign intervention, & we will have an honorable peace after all. Foreign intervention is the only thing that will put an end to this war. But the army of the Potomac will take Washington City [Washington, DC] & Baltimore [Maryland] to balance the losses of the south and to aid us in dictating equable terms of peace. Our whole army expects Genl. Lee[59] to attack Washington City and

---

[56] Machines ordered from England to manufacture cloth.

[57] Catherine Evelyn "Eva" King Baker, sister of Barrington S. King.

[58] Barrington, nicknamed Bubba, was the second child of Barrington S. and Bessie.

[59] Gen. Robert E. Lee, CSA, was the commander of the Army of Northern Virginia. Lee, a graduate of West Point and a career military man, left the US military two days after being offered command of the Federal armies by President Abraham Lincoln. With an inferior number of troops and material

all are willing to risk their lives in the effort. Meade[60] has got frightened and fallen back toward Centerville.[61] Our army is without doubt in as good fighting trim now this moment as it ever was and almost as strong numerically as it ever was. I think I will get back just in time to participate in the next great struggle for liberty & peace.   I am very glad Harris[62] is well & gives no trouble. I wish I could see him. Kiss him for me. Give much love to Dear Mother. Aunt Cliff[63] & all at home. I am sorry indeed that Mother has been suffering so much with headache and would advise Mother to come here for a change for a few weeks at any rate.

God Bless you Father & grant long life to you & an early peace to our country and a safe reunion of your family ever prays

Your Afte Son
B.S. King

---

resources, Lee defended Richmond and invaded the North twice. Two months before the Civil War ended, Lee was given command of all the Confederate armies (Boatner, *Civil War Dictionary,* 476).

[60] George Gordon Meade, Union commander, was the commander of the Army of the Potomac from just before Gettysburg to the end of the war. Meade commanded a brigade in the Peninsular campaign and in the Second Bull Run and commanded a division at Antietam and Fredericksburg. Other battles in which Meade saw action in include Chancellorsville, Gettysburg, Bristoe, and Mine Run campaigns. When a successor was sought for Hooker, Meade was chosen in place of John F. Reynolds, a more qualified leader (Boatner, *Civil War Dictionary,* 539).

[61] Centreville VA is located west of Washington, DC near Bull Run River.

[62] Harris was the oldest son of Barrington S. and Bessie King. He was left in Roswell with his grandparents.

[63] Aunt Cliff was Caroline Clifford Nephew, half sister of Barrington S. King's mother Catherine Margaret Nephew. Her husband was Joseph Clay Stiles.

During the later part of August, Cobb's Legion, Cavalry Battalion, was at Camp Gordon in Orange County, Virginia, located near the Orange Court House.[64]

The following letter gives a wonderful insight into the Georgia Gubernatorial candidates during the Civil War and how Barrington S. King viewed them.

Camp near Orange C.H.[65] Sept 18th 1863

My Dear Father

I wrote you a few lines last Sunday morning after "boots & saddle"[66] sounded in preparation to meet the Yankees then advancing upon us. I only wrote about some money to pay to different parties in Georgia which had been paid me here, to wit: C.A. Dunwoody[67] ($25-) Twenty Five dollars for A Souths[68] note for horse. G.A. Power[69] ($50-) Fifty dollars for C. Vaughn.[70] Mrs. J.S. Shaw ($125-) One hundred and Twenty Five dollars for J.S. Shaw.[71]

---

[64] Smedlund, *Camp Fires,* 139.

[65] Orange Courthouse VA is along the Orange & Alexandria Railroad south of the Rapidan River and southwest of Fredericksburg.

[66] "Boots and Saddle" was a bugle call directing soldiers to put on their riding boots and mount their horses.

[67] Charles A. Dunwoody is recorded as having served as a captain of the cavalry of the Roswell Battalion, Company B. According to this letter, he was with Cobb's Legion, Company E, as of September 1863.

[68] Amaziah South's. He served as a sergeant in Cobb's Legion, Company E.

[69] Aaron Powell served in Cobb's Legion, Company E.

[70] Claborn Vaughn served as a corporal in Cobb's Legion, Company E.

[71] J. Sidney Shaw served in Cobb's Legion, Company E.

Also Chambers[72] note to myself pd in full
    Stewarts[73] " " " " " "
    Dickersons[74] " " " " " " .

I would also be obliged to you if you would pay to Dr Geiger[75] the balance I owe him. I dont know the amnt as I had to destroy all letters for fear of having them captured I think it is in the neighborhood of $70- he will make out the account. We had on Sunday last one of the sharpest & meanest fights I ever was in The Yankees drove us as usual all day & all day myself & company were exposed to the hot fire of the sharpshooters. Lt. McDerment[76] was mortally wounded, Lowe[77] and Alexander[78] of Gwinnett [Gwinnett County, Georgia] slightly, and 4 horses killed were the casualties of my company. I most fervently thank God that I passed through all without a scratch. We fell back across the Rapidan at Racoon Ford[79] and Monday Tuesday & Wednesday we passed in occassional skirmishing across the river. Yesterday we moved up above Orange C.H. [Orange Court House] on Robertson & to day have been quietly in camp. We expect to have a plenty to do yet though. Dont know whether Genl Lee[80] will advance or not but think if Meade[81] advances we

---

[72] James B. Chambers served in Cobb's Legion, Company E.

[73] William T. M. Stewarts served in Cobb's Legion, Company E.

[74] Augustus C. Dickerson of Georgia served in Cobb's Legion, Company E.

[75] Charles A. Geiger.

[76] Marcus L. McDermont served in Cobb's Legion, Company E, as second lieutenant.

[77] John D. Lowe served in Cobb's Legion, Company E.

[78] David J. Alexander served in Cobb's Legion, Company E, or possibly Company F.

[79] Raccoon Ford on the Rapidan River is south of Culpeper Courthouse and due west of Fredericksburg VA.

[80] Gen. Robert E. Lee.

will whip him out. You are having pretty exciting times in Roswell I expect But as I heard some one say yesterday the people at home in Georgia are more scared at the thought of an advanced of the Yankees than the women are here.[82] If this many thousands of men yet in Georgia do their duty Rosecrans[83] will never come near Cobb Co [Georgia]. I dont feel at all uneasy about upper Georgia & I pray God you all may rest in peace and quiet at Roswell. The future looks dark & gloomy but every thing depends upon the people at home I am afraid we will have trouble in North Ca. [Carolina] by the submissionists & I very much fear we will in Georgia during the coming election for Gov. I see Hill[84] & out & out submissionist yes a real Union man is a candidate If he is elected Georgia is ruined. I would rather Brown[85] be in the Gubernatorial Chair his whole life than that 10 votes should be cast for Hill. I dont know what will become of our country unless our home people give the army every encouragement & support by words as well as actions. Our men become discouraged & cant fight when they hear of the many at home who are willing to submit. It is terrible to think what may become of us from want

---

[81] Gen. George Gordon Meade.

[82] Wives of the Confederate generals.

[83] William Starke Rosecrans, a Union general referred to as "Old Rosy" by his troops, led the Army of the Cumberland from 30 October 1862–20 October 1863 at Stones River, in the Tullahoma campaign, and at Chickamauga, where his defeat cost him his command (Boatner, *Civil War Dictionary,* 708).

[84] Benjamin H. Hill, prominent Georgia lawyer, was opposed to secession but signed the Ordinance of Secession for Georgia. He served as a Senator in the Confederate Congresses in 1861–1865. Following the war he was elected to the United States House of Representatives (1875–1877) and the United States Senate (1877–1882) (Boatner, *Civil War Dictionary,* 400).

[85] Joseph E. Brown was first elected governor of Georgia in 1857 and was reelected in 1859, 1861, and 1863. Brown disagreed with the way President Davis ran the government and the way he conducted war (Boatner, *Civil War Dictionary,* 91–92).

of fortitude in our people at home. God grant we may get come out of this struggle a pure people with an honorable peace upon our land. Give my love to dear Mother I am anxious to hear from home I have not heard anything of my little boy in a long time. God bless you ever prays

Your Afte. Son,
B.S. King

Camp near Orange C.H. Sept 25th 1863

My Dear Father

How greatly has God blessed our beloved country in giving us such a victory of arms over Resecranz.[86] The Tellegraph brings us news to day that "there are no armed Yankees south of the Tennessee river." How earnestly should we thank almighty God for this victory & for all his goodness towards us as a people & towards our family as individuals for we have had another terrible cavalry fight & I passed through all safe. I will tell you about our last fight. We were in saddle at 4 AM Tuesday to meet the enemy who had forced a crossing at Russels ford across the Roberson river[87] (which is our dividing line now to where it empties into the Rapidan there the Rapidan down to the Potomac) on the pike leading from Culpeper C.H. to Madison C.H.[88] We took blind roads leading through the woods until we struck the pike leading from Madison C.H. to Gordonsville[89] about 4 miles from the former place. Shortly after striking the Pike we met the enemy's advance Guard & the fight began. Our

---

[86] William Starke Rosecrans.

[87] Robertson River runs into the Rapidan River between Orange Courthouse and Culpeper Courthouse.

[88] Madison Courthouse is southwest of Culpeper Courthouse, opposite of the Robertson River.

[89] Gordonsville is south of Orange Courthouse along the railroad.

force was only Hamptons[90] Division consisting of Bakers,[91] Butlers[92] & Genes[93] Brigades (Butlers is Hamptons old Brigade in which our Regt. is) in all numbering about 2000 men (the summers campaign has cut us down terribly) Genes Brigade was on the left, ours centre, and Bakers right.

Our fighting began as all our Cavalry fights begin by dismounting & skirmishing. The fight soon became pretty warm & for some hours we held our ground although the enemys skirmishes were 4 times more than ours. about two oclock our sight flank fell back or was forced back then the left-flank retreated in almost a panic. Our centre remained firm till almost surrounded they fell back in good order to their horses which the mounted men of our Regt & the 2nd S.C. [South Carolina] held

---

[90] Gen. Wade Hampton, CSA, raised the Hampton Legion and led this unit during most of the Peninsular campaign. He was appointed brigadier general on 23 May 1862 and major general on 3 September 1863. He succeeded Stuart as commander of the cavalry corps after the battle of the Wilderness. Hampton and his forces fought at Haw's Shop, Sappony Church, Reams' Station, and Burgess Mill and blocked Sheridan's Trevilian Raid. He was appointed lieutenant general on 15 February 1865 (Boatner, *Civil War Dictionary,* 370–71).

[91] In 1861, Laurence Simmons Baker, CSA, was appointed lieutenant colonel 1st North Carolina Cavalry; he was promoted colonel in spring 1862 and fought under Lee from the Peninsula to Appomattox. Baker succeeded Hampton in command of his brigade near the end of the war (Boatner, *Civil War Dictionary,* 40).

[92] Matthew Calbraith Butler, C.S.A, was commissioned captain in the Hampton Legion and fought at First Bull Run. As major he fought in the Peninsular campaign. Promoted to colonel in August 1862, he commanded his regiment at Antietam and Fredericksburg. He lost his right foot at Brandy Station in June 1863. Upon returning to duty, he was promoted to brigadier general and commanded his brigade in the fighting around Richmond. On 17 September 1864, he was promoted to major general and joined Gen. Joseph E. Johnston in the Carolinas opposing Gen. William T. Sherman (Boatner, *Civil War Dictionary,* 110).

[93] Could not identify a Gene's or Jene's brigade.

the ground until every Regt had retreated down the Pike. The
sharp shooters of the enemy were within a hundred yds of us
pouring in the bullets our Loss was heavy. Col. Delinys[94] horse
was shot first in the flank & almost immediately after he himself
shot through the leg the same shot killing his horse instantly. I
was left in command of the Regt & as usual our Regt was placed
in the rear of our Retreating column with orders to charge should
the enemys cavalry show itself. With a small body of mounted
sharp shooters 50 yds in our rear to keep the enemys
sharpshooters from crowding us too closely we retreated down
the road at the slow walk for two hours, within from 1 to 4
hundred yds of the enemy who kept up a galling fire all the time.
I cant concieve how we escaped as we did for the enemy are all
armed with long range guns sighted for 1100 yds but can kill at
nearly a mile. Many a ball whized so close to me I could feel the
wind of it & I expected every moment to be struck in the back.
Many of ball passing me would kill or wound some man or horse
in front of me. It was a trying time to our Regt But every one
knows the material of which it is composed. At last the
sharpshooters pressed us so closely Genl Stuart[95] who had come
to the rear ordered me to make the rear Squadron charge them at
the command "Halt & "left about wheel" the Regt obeyed as

---

[94] William G. Delony, Cobb's Legion, Company C.

[95] James Ewell Brown "Jeb" Stuart, CSA general and cavalry leader, had
served on the frontier in Indian fighting and had volunteered with Robert E.
Lee during John Brown's raid to Harpers Ferry. He was commissioned
lieutenant colonel of the Virginia Infantry and named Captain of CSA cavalry
two weeks later. He rose in rank quickly, becoming brigadier general 24
September 1861 and major general 25 July 1862, taking command of the
cavalry in the Army of Northern Virginia at that time. Having led his troops at
such battles as Fredericksburg, Chancellorsville, Gettysburg, the Wilderness,
and Spotsylvania, as well as his two "rides around McClellan," Stuart died of
wounds he received at Yellow Tavern 11 May 1864 (Boatner, *Civil War
Dictionary*, 812–13).

promptly as on the drill "First squadron *charge*" & away they
went down the road. the Yankees some dropped their guns &
jumped the fence on one side & others ran into the woods firing
into us as we came up & then running still farther away. I halted
them before they should run too far into the enemys line & from
that time we retreated in safety to Rapidan river and from thence
went up the river to meet a large force which were on their way
to Charlottesville night coming on put an end to a small artillery
duel & the next morning being reinforced during the night by Fitz
Lee's[96] division the Yankees retreated and we followed them up
driving them across the Roberson river again recovering our
former lines. & All is quiet again. Our loss was 17 wounded
(privates) 3 officers, Killed 3 privates. To our great regret Col
Deleny,[97] our Surgeon and 4 of our wounded while going to the
rear were captured. He is a great loss to our Regt & our whole
cavalry division for all the cavalry force know that Cobb Legion
with Col Deleny leading them can never be run by Yankees. It is
a great honor for me to lead a regiment with such a reputation
But a few more such fights & we placed next the enemy & there
will be nothing left of us. We can only mount 140 men for duty
now. We lost nearly 100 horses in the last two fights most of
them the best horses of the Regt. It is not right to make us the

---

[96] Fitzhugh "Fitz" Lee, CSA general, was a nephew of Robert E. Lee and of
James M. Mason. Commissioned as a first lieutenant, he served on Ewell's and
J. E. Johnston's staffs during the Peninsular campaign. Lee was promoted to
lieutenant colonel of the 1st Virginia Cavalry in August 1861, a colonel the
following March, and brigadier general 24 July 1862. His cavalry brigade saw
action at South Mountain, Antietam, Gettysburg, on the Dumfries and
Occoquan raids, and guarded Jackson's movements at Chancellorsville. On 3
August 1863, Lee was promoted to major general, before he was twenty-eight,
and he led his command at Spotsylvania and supported Lt. Gen. Jubal A. Early
in August 1864 in the Shanendoah River Valley. He succeeded Hampton as
senior cavalry commander in the Army of Northern Virginia (Boatner, *Civil
War Dictionary,* 475).

[97] William G. Delony, Cobb's Legion, Company C.

shield of other Regts whose reputation is not so good as ours. We foiled the enemys plans entirely. His object avowed were to take our Rail Road between us & Lynchburg & Richmond. But for the stubborn fight we gave them holding them in check until we were reinforced & they would have made a big raid on a grand scale. They had brought over 18000 cavalry & 26 pieces of artilery. Meade is afraid to advance and there will be no big fight until Genl Lee Advances which no one knows when will be. I had two men wounded in my company both from Gwinnett [County, Georgia]. I thank God for the preservation of my life & shielding me from all harm through so much danger. Upper Georgia is more safe for this winter & I most earnestly pray our Father to grant us peace before another summers campaign begins. It is my firm conviction that this is the last campaign of this bloody war, & that a bright day is now already dawning upon our beloved country Bessie is still with Eva[98] & is under treatment of Dr Waddel. Give much love to dear mother & all at home. May God bless you & permit us all to meet when this war ends ever prays

Your Aftc Son,
B.S. King

As previously mentioned, Barrington S. King had worked out a system of receiving money from soldiers and having his father pay their wives, allowing King to have extra spending money on hand. The following is an appendage to the previous letter regarding more financial exchanges.

---

[98] Catherine Evelyn "Eva" King Baker was Barrington S. King's sister.

                                                        25 Sept
P.S.   Dear Father

    Several of my men wishing to send money to their wives I recd it as I wanted some for my wife & for myself as I cant begin to live on my pay. They gave me more than I actually want but will not waste it. I told them to write to the parties to call on you for it. Please pay & charge to me.

P.G. Allbritten[99] to pay J.L. Allbritten

                              J.L. Allbritten [signature] $80.00

J L Stewart[100] to pay note for horse   Entd 31 Dec $25.00

Do "" " " Mrs. J L Stewart   Martha J. Stewart [signature] $60.00

A South[101] " " Mrs. A. South   Nancy South [signature] $100.00

P Coleman[102] with R.B. King[103] Mrs. P. Coleman   Sandy   Coleman   X
[her mark] $100.00

R.H. Willbanks[104] " " note for horse Entd 31 Dec $20.00

Do Wm. Young to pay Mrs. R.H. Willbanks   M.A. Willbanks
   $40.00

Elijah Linsey " " Note for horse   Entd 31 Dec $25.00

A.C. Dickerson[105] Danl Wright Mrs. A.C. Dickerson Mrs. Dickerson
[signature] $120.00

Allen Grimes[106] [illegible] "John Grimes[107]   Elisa Grimes X [her mark]
   $60.00

---

[99] Pleasant G. Allbritten served in Cobb's Legion, Company E.

[100] J. Lafayette Stewart served in Cobb's Legion, Company E, as a sergeant.

[101] Amaziah South was a sergeant in Cobb's Legion, Company E.

[102] P. Newton Coleman served in Cobb's Legion, Company E.

[103] Ralph Brown King was a brother of Barrington S. King.

[104] Richard H. Willbanks served in Cobb's Legion, Company E.

[105] Augustus C. Dickerson of Georgia served in Cobb's Legion, Company E.

[106] Allen T. Grimes served in Cobb's Legion, Company E.

James A. Voss[108] [illegible] " Mrs. James A Voss Rebecca Voss X [her mark] $200.00
Mrs J S Shaw[109] $125 Paid
      $830.00
Wm C. Vaughn[110]——   50 Paid

In looking over my accounts I find that all the notes have been pd off. But I may have neglected to tell you the amnts to credit with All except A.J. Foremans[111] and J.H. Bone.[112] Their horses died & I could not retain the wages only for the amnts as here to fore stated. McDerment's[113] note I had nothing more to do with after Mc became a comd [commanding] officer. Ramseys[114] note I have done all I promised to do & will leave it for Ramsey and Arnold to settle. I think though you may as well pay it as Ramsey has no right to retain the money. Henry Smith[115] has no horse and I cannot draw his wages unless he was here. He is a brave little soldier through and deserves a good horse.

Your letter of the 10th concerning notes came after the men had drawn their money. South,[116] Wilbanks,[117] Linsey[118] &

---

[107] John Grimes served in the Cavalry, Roswell Battalion, Company C and Company A.

[108] James A. Voss of Georgia served in Cobb's Legion, Company E.

[109] J. Sidney Shaw served in Cobb's Legion, Company E.

[110] Claborn Vaughn served as a corporal in Cobb's Legion, Company E.

[111] A. J. Foreman (or Freeman) served in Cobb's Legion, Company E.

[112] Joseph H. Bone served in Cobb's Legion, Company E.

[113] Marcus L. McDermont was a second lieutenant in Cobb's Legion, Company E.

[114] S. T. Ramsey served in Cobb's Legion, Company E.

[115] Henry W. Smith was a corporal in Cobb's Legion, Company E.

[116] Amaziah South.

[117] Richard H. Willbanks served in Cobb's Legion, Company E.

[118] Elijah Linsey served in Cobb's Legion, Company E.

Stewart[119] only have pd it back. Owens,[120] Mitchel,[121] Drake,[122] & Coleman,[123] did not draw money being absent, Perryman[124] & Paden[125] have failed to pay it back. I will hereafter retain the wages of the horse. I will remain in command of the Regt for some weeks Col Young[126] is expected back daily but will command the Brigade until Genl Butler[127] recovers from his wound. I have not heard how McDerment[128] is to day but hope he is getting well he was better last monday when I heard last. I am much obliged for the investment you made for me in Cotton. I sincerely hope the Yankees will never give you occasion to use the defenses of Roswell. Love to dear Mother & all

Your Afte. Son,
B.S. King

Camp near Fredricksburg [Fredericksburg, Virginia]
Nov 6th 1863

My Dear Father,

We are still at this place to guard the tearing up and running of the Rail Road iron on the other side of the river. Day before yesterday the enemy with 10 Regts of Cavalry & 3 Batteries (4

---

[119] J. Lafayette Stewart served as a sergeant in Cobb's Legion, Company E.

[120] Ira W. Owens served in Cobb's Legion, Company E.

[121] Roland P. Mitchell served in Cobb's Legion, Company E.

[122] James S. Drake served in Cobb's Legion, Company E.

[123] P. Newton Coleman served in Cobb's Legion, Company E.

[124] Thomas J. Perryman served in Cobb's Legion, Company E.

[125] Samuel D. Paden served in Cobb's Legion, Company E.

[126] Pierce Manning Butler Young, CSA.

[127] Matthew Calbraith Butler, CSA.

[128] Marcus L. McDermont.

pieces each) of Artillery drove us across the river. We contested
every inch of ground though giving the working party time to
escape with waggons, tools & c [etc.]. If they had been brave &
acted as our Brigade would have done that is just charged right
down upon us there would have been no more "Cobb Legion
Cavry" to the end of this war. They were afraid to do it though
they knew ours was the Regt they had to continue against. It was
high tide when our men reached the river and all had to swim
their horses over. It was *very* exciting & the suspense very
painful as we expected the yankees would charge down and open
on us in the act of crossing. But we got over safe every man &
dismounting very quickly our men were all in the rifle pits
guarding the fords & the horses hid before the head of their
column made its appearance. Yankee Brig Genl Custer[129] was in
advance & as he came in long range of our guns our men opened
on them so warmly that he galloped back and told the citizens he
"did not know we had infantry over here". They took good care
not to come within range again although they had force enough
to have eat us up They were afraid too of firing upon us with
artillery for fear of bringing down Genl Stuart[130] in their rear.
They paraded in front of us though a force of 4 Regts & eight
pieces of artillery marching out towards the Rail Road & then
marching back towards Bealeton the route they came in from.

---

[129] George Armstrong Custer, Union general, was an outstanding cavalry
leader and was named brigadier general 29 June 1863 at the age of twenty-three
and major general on 15 April 1865 at the age of twenty-five. Custer missed
only one battle of the Army of the Potomac during the Civil War and led his
cavalry with particularly skillful tactics through Gettysburg, Yellow Tavern,
Winchester, Fishers Hill, and Five Forks. Although wounded only once during
the Civil War, he had eleven horses killed under him. Custer lacked the
abilities of organizing artillery, infantry, and cavalry, which is demonstrated
by the events at Little Big Horn, 25 June 1876 (Boatner, *Civil War Dictionary*,
216).
[130] James Ewell Brown "Jeb" Stuart, CSA.

The citizens say they seemed much alarmed for fear of an attack by Genl Stuart from above. Our pickets are again 15 miles on the other side of the river & our scouts report no enemy nearer than white oak ridge about 20 miles from here.

These shirmishes are very annoying and although the danger is less than in a "big fight" yet the casualties of a whole campaign will in our Regt equal that of any infantry Regt in service. The worst of it is we are almost continually at these shirmishes which use us up men and horses pretty severely. I hope though as we will have reinforcements soon we will have a little resting spell. I am (by promotion of Genl Young[131]) major of our Regt now. You have by previous letters heard of the death of our brave & noble Col Deleny.[132] I feel his loss very very much and am exceedingly sorry to say I take my recent promotion as Lt Col by his death I have no military ambitions only to serve my country in the best manner and to the best of my ability & would have been contented to remain major to the end of this war if the lives of the other field Officers could have been spared. We have had official information of Col Delenys death mortification of the knee took place & he died on the 2nd of October in Washington.

Horses are a pretty heavy expense in cavalry I have only two that are of any account for service and one of them my black which I bought last spring is almost used up so that I will have to send him off to recruit. I will be obliged to buy another horse. I have two in Staunton, neither of which are fit for service, but for sale will bring fine prices. I expect to sell them for at least $2500 for the two. I wish if you or any of my brothers know of a good horse with a good *walk trot & gallop* you would buy it for me. A detail will go home for horses next week & I will get a care ful man of my old company to bring him

---

[131] Pierce Manning Butler Young, CSA.

[132] William G. Delony, Cobb's Legion, Company C.

out for me. Horses are as high here as anywhere & none fit for cavalry can be bought at any price.

It will be the 1st of Jan before the detail gets back & I will I expect by that time be back from my leave of absence which I expect to get early next month to take my wife home.[133] And to see dear Mother yourself & all. I am in hopes my wife is now perfectly well if so the trip to Virginia is well repaid. Give my love to dear Mother & all a home and may God bless you all & spare our lives to meet next month pray

Your Afte Son
B.S. King

P.S. In my letter to you some weeks ago requesting you to pay certain amounts to persons mentioned I forgot to put down $125 to pay Mrs. J. S. Shaw from her husband, J. S. Shaw[134] at least Shaw says his wife told him you said I had not mentioned it in my letter. If you have not paid it please pay it to her. Paid 19 Nov

Also C. Vanghn[135] says the $50 I requested you to pay Mr Power, Mr. Power says he can not get or you wont pay him. If you have not pd it please pay the amnt $50 to Mrs. C. Vanghn. Paid 2 Dec 1863 $50

The following letter was written by Barrington King to inform his son, Barrington S. King, of the death of another of his sons, Thomas Edward King. Thomas had left his role as Captain in command of the Roswell battalion on 12 September 1863. He was killed 19 September 1863 at the Battle of Chickamauga as a captain in the Confederate State Army. Earlier that same year,

---

[133] He was to escort Bessie to Roswell from Virginia.

[134] J. Sidney Shaw served in Cobb's Legion, Company E.

[135] Claborn Vaughn served as a corporal in Cobb's Legion, Company E.

28 February 1863, his wife Mary "Marie" Reid Clemons had spoken of him not being able to fight in the army and what a great disappointment that was to him.

9 P.M.
Roswell 16th Nov 1863

Major B.S. King
Cav: Cobb Legion Richmond

My dear Son Yours of the 6th Novr recd this morning, & thankful to learn that you continue well, & have escaped thus far in the war— the death of your Brother T.E. King[136] was a sad blow to me, but he fell on a noble cause: done with the trials of this life, & now happy forever in heaven. God above knows what will be the result of this unnatural war— we have justice on our side, but deserve sever chastisement *for our sins as a nation*: May we all repent of short comings on duty, and look to God for his blessings—otherwise every thing dark and gloomy. Rather than submit to Yankee rule—trust the Confederacy will resist to the last : better loose every thing, than our liberty. Ralph[137] is a captain of a company in Augusta lately formed there as home guards—Clifford[138] is in Savannah in the staff of Genl Colston.[139] Your Brother James has the command on this place. We are happy to learn that Bessy has improved in health—

---

[136] Thomas Edward King.

[137] Ralph Brown King, brother of Barrington S. King.

[138] Barrington S. King's youngest brother, Clifford Alonzo King.

[139] Raleigh Edward Colston, CSA Colston was a graduate of the Virginia Military Institute and a professor there when the war began. He obtained the rank of brigadier general 24 December 1861, and he participated in many significant battles of the Civil War. During 1863 he was stationed in Savannah GA (Clement Evans, *Confederate Military History*, vol. 3 [Atlanta: Confederate Publishing Company, 1899]).

Harris[140] continues well & we try to train him properly. You say nothing about the servant Lysy, hope he has been of service to you—he promised to you satisfaction. I have not been well of late & Mother has been suffering from headache— we expect to make a visit next week to Savannah to be absent a few weeks : trusting the change will benefit us both, happy to meet you here in December God willing. Tuesday 17th— The mail about closing— in you letter requesting us to pay several persons nothing was mentioned about paying Mrs J S Shaw[141] $125 & $50 to Mrs C. Vaughan[142]: some few have not yet called, those that call have always been paid. Dr Geiger[143] has gone to Wilmington to see after the Machinery from England, some has arrived there & he is making an arrangement to operate in Macon,[144] I paid him the amt he claimed from you $119 45/100 for 1/3 cost & expences, balance & took his net. It was more than you said in your letter. There is no telling what Genl Bragg[145] is after— it is said that Longstreet[146] has gone [illegible]

---

[140] Barrington S. and Bessie's oldest son.

[141] J. Sidney Shaw served in Cobb's Legion, Company E.

[142] Claborn Vaughn served in Cobb's Legion, Company E.

[143] Charles A. Geiger.

[144] Macon GA is 80 miles south of Atlanta.

[145] Gen. Braxton Bragg, CSA, was a career military man, resigning in 1856. Bragg was appointed brigadier general on 7 March 1861. On 12 April 1862 he was made a full general and on 27 June he replaced Beauregard as commander of the Army of Tennessee. He was relieved from command by Joseph E. Johnston after Chickamauga and Chattanooga, returning to Richmond as military advisor to President Davis. He was with Davis when he was captured in Georgia (Boatner, *Civil War Dictionary*, 78).

[146] Gen. James "Pete" Longstreet, CSA, appointed brigadier general 17 June 1861 and major general 7 October 1861. His mistakes at Fair Oaks and Seven Pines caused the operation to fail. A similar fate took place in the Second Bull Run. However, he fought well at Antietam and was promoted to lieutenant general 9 October 1862. Perhaps his greatest failure was to agree with the offensive attacks at Gettysburg and in turn to delay in attacking on

East Tennessee to drive out Barnsides,[147] & get supplies for the army should Bragg fall back, this portion of our state would be overran by the Vandalls [vandals], & they would destroy every thing— we hope for the best. Horses are scarce on this quarter & high. Dr Stetes got a first rate one in Atlanta cost $1100— well make inquery [inquiry] and see what can be done for you. Mother & all join in love to you— place your trust in God my son, and may his blessing attend you ever prays your affn Father

B. King

Camp near Tolersville [Virginia]
Nov 26th 1863

Misters Kent Paine & Co

Richmond Va.
Dr Sirs

Mrs King [Bessie] may call on you for money which she may require. Please let her have what she may wish taking her reciept for same.

Very Resptly [respectfully] Yours
B.S. King
Lt Col Cavry Cobb Legion

---

the second day. This brought the widest criticism after the war. He was sent to support Bragg in the west. He was seriously wounded on 6 May 1864 during the Wilderness campaign (Boatner, *Civil War Dictionary*, 490–91).

[147] Ambrose E. Burnside, U.S., had served in the United States military, resigning in 1853. He entered the Civil War as colonel of the 1st Rhode Island Volunteers. Burnside received promotions to brigadier general and major general and twice refused to command Army of Potomac, accepting the third time it was offered. However, Burnside was relieved of duty after the failure of Fredericksburg. After serving a short time as the commander of the Army of the Ohio, he returned to the east as commander of the IX Corps, fighting in the Battle of the Wilderness, Spotsylvania, North Anna, Totopotomoy, and Bethesda Church. For mishandling troops in the Petersburg mine assault, Burnside was relieved from duty again (Boatner, *Civil War Dictionary*, 107).

During early and mid-December, the Confederate government was stressing the defense of Atlanta. In a letter dated 14 December 1863, Colonel M. H. Wright wrote that he had about 1,800 men with his main strength being the local force, which worked in various shops as mechanics. In Roswell there were "150 men, armed with two pieces of artillery, and 40 mounted men, to guard that ford."[148] These men were employees of the Roswell Manufacturing Company and were under the command of Captain James Roswell King, brother of B. S. King, whom Wright referred to as "a very fine officer."[149] James had replaced Thomas as commander of this battalion.

The following letter tells how long it has been since King has been home and gives a description of the purpose of the visit, which is the machinery imported from England to aid in the manufacturing of cloth.

Hd Ass [Head Assistant] Cobb Legion Cavry
Camp near "Hamiltons Crossing" Dec 28th 1863
Col R.H. Chilton A. & I.G.
Army Northern Va
Col

I have the honor to make application for Thirty days *Leave of absence* to visit my home in Georgia. It is over one year since I was last at home.

I have during the past summer with the consent & approbation of the War Dpt had imported from England machinery of an important character for the purpose of manufacturing "card clothing" for Cotton & woolen mills, of

---

[148] *OR*, ser. 1, vol. 31, pt. 3, p. 821.

[149] Ibid., 822.

which *all* the mills of the Confederacy are *much* in need. The machines are not in operation, my *personal attention* being necessary to put them in full & successful operation, thereby advancing the interest of our *whole* country, as well as *personal*. By the Act of Congress, I could be exempted from all military duty, to remain at home & superintend said machines. But my *first & greatest* duty is for my country, and all I ask, is to allowed the above time *now* that I may be able to serve my *own* interest as well as my *country's*.

I am Col
Very Resptly [respectfully]
Your Obt Svt [obedient servant]
B.S. King
Lt Col Cobb Legion Cavry

The following is a form for a leave of absence.

Adjutant and Inspector General's Office,
Richmond, Jany 16th, 1864

SPECIAL ORDERS,
No. 13

X   _____   X   X

XVIIII The Leave of absence heretofore granted Lieut Col. *B.S. King* Cobbs Legion Cavalry, is extended ten days.

By command of the Secretary of War.
Lieut Col. B.S. King   Jno.   [John] Withers,
Thro Genl LJ Gartrul[150] MC.   Assistant Adjutant General

---

[150] Lucius Jeremiah Gartrell, C.S.A, had been elected to the state legislature and US Congress prior to the war. He resigned his seat when Georgia

This leave of absence appears to have been extended to enable King to organize new recruits as empowered by Major-General J. E. B. Stuart. In a letter dated 28 January 1864, Stuart informed General S. Cooper of the orders he gave Brigadier General Butler and King due to the large number of men serving in the state regiments as a result of the conscript law.[151]

After his furlough, Barrington S. King returned to the front with new recruits to face a fierce summer of battles. Summer 1864 brought a moral blow for the soldiers of Cobb's Legions, as the Union forces fought in North Georgia and took Atlanta, leading to the Union occupation of the soldier's homeland.

The next correspondence is dated 24 March 1864. It is a printed receipt form for the purchase of Confederate Bonds, indicating that Barrington S. King purchased bonds with 300 dollars in Confederate Treasury Notes.

In early April 1864, the legion was camped in Camp Marion in Spotsylvania County, Virginia, near Fredericksburg, Virginia.

Camp near Chesterfield Station April 21st 1864

My Dear Father

Your letter of the 7th was recd last Saturday & dear Mothers of the 12th recd yesterday. I have been very busy during the week or would have written you sooner. I regret much that the

---

seceded. He was commissioned as colonel of the 7th Georgia and led his regiment at First Bull Run, where his sixteen-year-old son was killed. He obtained the rank of brigadier general 22 August 1864 and commanded his brigade of Georgia Reserves in South Carolina (Boatner, *Civil War Dictionary*, 326).

[151] *OR,* ser. 1, vol. 33, p. 1125.

draft on Kent Paine & Co[152] was delayed so long on the route. I gave it in payment for a horse, as I thought in plenty time to be paid in the old currency, as that was my object in buying at the time, that I might be paid in that way. And the draft I gave Vaughn[153] on you was money borrowed from him to pay for the same horse, expecting of course to pay it back to Vaughn in the same currency I borrowed. In fact Vaughn came to me asking me to take $600- and give him a draft on you as he was going home & might lose it. It was my intention & am almost certain I said on the draft "payable in the currency of date previous to April 1st 1864." Did you see the draft? or did Vaughn only tell you about it. I hope you have not pd him only with the Old currency & at its value of before 1st April. I would be glad to have the $600 draft on Kent Paine & Co pd in 4 pr ct [percent] bonds rather than pay in the new currency.

My wife [Bessie] is comfortably fined in a house about 12 miles from camp. Baby[154] & herself quite well. I was considerably disappointed when she first came on that Harris was not with her But on consideration think now it is well he is at home with his grand parents with whom he is contented, happy and safe. Bessie will remain with me until am ordered into the field when she will go to Richmond & remain there until the campaign is decided which will in all probability be by the 1st of June. We are not certain yet whether our Brigade will go on duty before the 1st of June. Our horses have gone down to skeletons our whole Brigade numbers 83 servicable horses for duty. & upwards of 1600 unservicable horses. Ours is the only cavalry Brigade that has had no rest since the begining of the campaign 10th May 1863. We are expecting orders now every day which will either "send us below Richmond to recruit" or "to be kept at Richmond as the

---

[152] A store in Virginia where Barrington S. and Bessie shopped.

[153] Claborn Vaughn served as a corporal in Cobb's Legion, Company E.

[154] Barrington was the second child of Barrington S. and Bessie.

Brigade ordered by Genl Bragg for that purpose" or sent to Fredrisburg [Fredericksburg, Virginia] when all the cavalry on the right flank is collecting to feed on the grass now springing up & to be ready to move when the campaign opens. I would be perfectly satisfied to do the hardest duties a soldier ever yet performed if our Regt could only put into the field 400 men well mounted so that we could add fresh laurels to our command with those nobly won on so many hard fought battle fields. But to go on duty at the opening of the campaign with 75 or an 100 men we can not do justice to ourselves or command & our service to the government will be nothing. But if they will only give us to the 1st of June with good feeding & grazing we will have in our Regt 400 men well mounted, and a Regt that will not fail in the performance of any duty which could be expected of it. It will not be many days before the hard booming of the cannon will be heard in our front one week more of dry weather & our army will make a forward move. A great many changes are taking place that the papers will not speak off [of] and of which I will have to remain silent. When the campaign does begin though, Genl Grant[155] will find he has another man to Genl Bragg[156] to cope with & our noble Lee[157] will be ready to meet him at every point yes & to attack & press him too. I regret from my heart the condition of our Brigade I hate to think we may not be in this campaign or rather in the 1st fight upon which so much depends

---

[155] Gen. Ulysses Simpson Grant, U.S., was appointed brigadier general at the beginning of the war and gained national attention with his success at Fort Henry, Fort Donelson, Shiloh, and Vicksburg. He was promoted to lieutenant general on 9 March 1864 and made general in chief of the armies of the United States on 12 March 1864 due to his victories around Chattanooga. He consequently took over the strategic direction of the war (Mark Mayo Boatner III, *The Civil War Dictionary*, rev. ed. [New York: David McKay Company, Inc.] 352–52).

[156] Gen. Braxton Bragg, CSA.

[157] Gen. Robert E. Lee, CSA.

and then too I hate to think we may be forced in to do the duty of a Brigade & keep up the reputation of our old Hamptons[158] Brigade with men not numbering more than 2 good squadrons. If the Yankees meet us and give us battle this spring great & terrible will this fight be Oh! that God in his omnipotence & in mercy ordain & bring about an honorable peace without the shedding of any more human blood. But as far as human eyes can see this cannot be the fight is inevitable may God Grant us the victory. If I should be among the number to fall in our final struggle I beg dear Mother & yourself to bear with my wife in her grief which from her disposition I am afraid will be ungovernable and as long as you both live to be a Father & a mother to her and my children. I do not look forward with the least dread or uneasiness to this campaign. I believe it to be the last of this war which has delayed our fair lives with blood and I believe if I fall it is the will of God & that through His Son I will inherit a home among the blessed.

I am very glad to hear my dear little Hatter[159] is such a good boy & gives you no trouble. I know he can not be anything but happy with two such good grand parents to care for him. I expect he will learn to spell & read very quickly under Miss Hamiltons teaching. But whenever he gets tired of it or wishes to stay at home please dont force him to go. We have heard nothing from Aunt Cliff.[160] Eva[161] has written all well with her. You will probably have fighting in upper Georgia before long. Here we all

---

[158] Hampton's Brigade, Gen. Wade Hampton, CSA.

[159] Harris, Barrington and Bessie's oldest child, was left with his grandparents in Roswell.

[160] Aunt Cliff was Caroline Clifford Nephew, half sister of Barrington S. King's mother Catherine Margaret Nephew. Her husband was Joseph Clay Stiles.

[161] Catherine Evelyn "Eva" King Baker was the sister of Barrington S. King.

expect Johnson[162] will have an easy victory & recover Genl as Grant[163] has drawn heavily on the western army for reenforcements. If the campaign opens in our favor I will send Bessie to Staunton, [Virginia] where boarding is cheaper. In Richmond she will board at Mrs Jennetts [unknown] the place where Ida was when she died.

I am afraid that Yarn you sent me is lost I regret it very much as I intended making it support my family here this summer. Martha behaves herself very well. Clara had better be hired out for the present any way.[164]

I will write to Mother next week give much love to her in which Bessie joins with me the same for yourself and kisses for our Hadder.

May God bless you both & keep you from all harm permitting us to meet in safety when this war ends prays

Your Aftc Son

B.S. King

---

[162] Gen. Joseph E. Johnston, CSA, was named brigadier general on 14 May 1861 and given Harpers Ferry. He had been a senior officer in the United States Army and felt he should also have that rank in the Confederate Army. This caused trouble between he and President Jefferson Davis, resulting in Davis's having him removed from his post after being injured twice at Seven Pines. Their differences of opinion continued after Johnston returned to duty five months later as the leader of the army in the west, causing the failure of the Confederate Army at Stones River, Vicksburg, Chickamauga, and Chattanooga. He was then given the command of the Army of Tennessee with orders to reorganize it. In the Atlanta Campaign, he dropped back before Gen. William T. Sherman's larger forces. For this he was replaced with Gen. John B. Hood on 17 July 1864 (Boatner, *Civil War Dictionary,* 441).

[163] Gen. Ulysses Simpson Grant, U.S.

[164] Martha and Clara were slaves, or servants as the Kings like to refer to them, and were probably staying with Bessie and the baby.

The following letter is from Bessie to Barrington S. King's mother.

Letter No 5.

Richmond May 10th/64-

My Dearest Mother,

Well can I imagine the suspense which you all endure at home; while awaiting tidings from your boy. Think of my setting here in Richmond, not 60 miles from him, & now in 5 days, have heard not a word! On Friday, he sent a Telegram, telling me to remain here until further news— But I never got it! It was sent, but the boy carried it to *another* Reads[165]—& it *cannot* be found. Since then, he has been fighting, but not one *word* have I heard. There is one thing which you may not know at home and that is, the mails from this point & all which come here have not been opened for 5 or 6 days— All the P.O. clerks, have been off with the City Ball—& good service have they rendered too.[166] But *what* could *they* do, in the field compared with the great misery & anxiety which is felt, all thro [through] the Confederacy? Of course, it would not do, to publish this fact, for the benefit of Beast Butler,[167] but *it is* a fact.

---

[165] Bessie was staying with Dr. or Rev. C. H. Read in Richmond VA, and Barrington's messages to her were sent to another household with the same surname.

[166] The post offices in Richmond appear to have been closed, allowing the postal workers to aid the Confederacy on the front.

[167] Benjamin Franklin Butler, U.S., was a major general. He was famous for capturing Fort Hatteras and Fort Clark in North Carolina, giving him the reputation of being a strategist. He occupied New Orleans after Farragut's fleet had reduced its defenses. He was famous for having William Mumford hung for removing the Union flag from the mint and for his "Woman Order" against the women of New Orleans. According to sources, his nickname was "spoons" for allegedly stealing silverware (Boatner, *Civil War Dictionary,* 109).

We all know how every soldier as sorry as a fight is over, writes to his *homes*, of his safety. & now there are piles. of mail matter here, untouched- for days— A pretty exciting time, we have had of it—& alas, *still* have, for we are beset one all sides—Grant[168] on the front & the Beast[169] at Drurys Bluff, which is *just* 8 miles from B. [Barrington] & raiders on the Central R. Road. the *alarms* Bell tolling for hours yesterday & Sunday. until I really felt nervous- & then too, no news from Barrington, which was such an even *present* anxiety that other things dwindle into insignificance. And now, we are waiting with fear & trembling, news from upper Geo. But Providence has so signally blessed us- that I hope & pray for the best.

Poor Genl. Jenkins[170] of S. Carolina was carried thro about this times yesterday. ~~with~~ on his way home. I have met a gentleman who had served under him & he speaks of him as *so noble* brave & *good*—& told me of his *four* little Boys- the eldest not over 6- years— he was about 30—& Genl. Slofford [unknown], too, was buried at Hollywood,[171] yesterday. *he* leaves a wife & *9 children* & his eldest son, a boy of 16—is here, having served with his father. Knowing these facts, & seeing wounded men, brought in daily, & hourly, its a terribly trying time—& no news from my husband.

---

[168] Gen. Ulysses Simpson Grant, U.S.

[169] Benjamin Franklin Butler, U.S.

[170] Gen. Micah Jenkins, CSA, was commissioned colonel of 5th South Carolina and was appointed brigadier general 22 July 1862. He was wounded at Second Bull Run. He commanded his brigade at Fredericksburg, Chickamauga, Knoxville, and the Wilderness. He was fatally wounded in the Wilderness by a Confederate soldier on 6 May 1864 (Boatner, *Civil War Dictionary,* 435).

[171] Hollywood Cemetery in Richmond VA is the burial place of US Presidents James Monroe and John Tyler as well as Confederate President Jefferson Davis, Gen. J. E. B. Stuart, and Gen. George Pickett. There are some 18,000 Confederate soldiers, including more than 2,000 that were removed from the Gettysburg battlefield, also buried here. The southern section of the cemetery overlooks the James River.

Wednesday 11th

Something, I dont know what, possessed me with the idea, of hearing from B—[Barrington] & notwithstanding the heat, I took the long walk down to the Post, & Telegraph Offices- at the latter, they were *just* this writing off my Dispatch, the ink was not dry. Barrington says, "he is safe & this for thank God, victorious"— The operation, really seemed delighted, to give it to me. I used to besiege him every day. & Dr. Read is often at him. After I read it the gentleman at the Desk, requested permission to read it. & of course I handed it to him.

Thursday.

Yesterday, we have heavy fighting in 6 miles of us—at 6- in the morning— Three heavy columns, of Grants cavalry which Genls Stuart & Fitz Lee,[172] fought them, & drove them down, & to day, we were roused at 4 in the morning- I counted over 100 cannon reports, in one half hour— I staid up until 5- & as I had passed a very restless night, went back to bed & to sleep— They have kept it up until now—3 PM—tho at longer intervals, they are only 4 miles from us now- & report say we have them *surrounded* (the Raiding party) *entirely*, & they are fighting *despesately*— Poor Genl. Stuart, is mortally wounded & while protecting us from these *very* creatures. He is lying only a few doors from us- & they (the Surgeons) say his strong constitution, is *all* they keeps him alive, even for a few hours—& he may linger on for two or three days. His Chief of Artillery was mortally wounded. a very gallant Officer, & one whom I knew— Only think, we have lost 8 *Maj* Genls—& I dont *know* how many Cols., Lt. Cols. & Captains, also not to *mention* the poor privates— But the Officers we have lost, are of *unprecedenteds* numbers—& the fight we *fear* is not *yet* over. Every firing of the big guns, jars the house. as I write, & they come generally about 2 reports, every 5 minutes—generally oftener. I don't know how

---

[172] Fitzhugh "Fitz" Lee, CSA general.

to believe it myself, but I am calmly, *coolly* writing—& have been hard at work all day- Dear mother your letter of the 28rd of April has just come. The mail being opened for the first time in about 5 days— I think you *very* much indeed for it—but am sorry you wrote, when feeling so badly; & you dont know how delighted I was with it, & so much about *dear* little *Harris* & *home*. Bless his heart, it makes me long for the time when I can be with you all once more. Your letter was so sweet, so like *yourself,* that I took a good hearty cry over it—& it has done me good too— I am exceedingly anxious to Telegraph you, but it is not possible yet. While the line to Petersburg [Petersburg, Virginia] is cut, so often & the Yankees have the line. I trust you will *understand* it, while you hear nothing, for you know dear Mother, I will relieve you anxiety just as *soon* as it is possible— They would not take the Telegrams where it came, I wanted to forward it at once, as B. had said— But they told me it could not go for the present. The streets have a quiet deserted sort of look. & now & then, you will see a group of Ladies, on a door step, hailing each other (there are no men in the city)—for the news, & oh! its well our bumps of credulity have been tried before, or we would certainly go crazy. if we *did* believe one half. I wait for "R.E. Lees" signature, & *then know* its true, but trust little else.

Friday Night

I sent your Dispatch yesterday. & today, had another—still safe & *well*—tho only *one* day later, than yours, it has been *two days* hunting me up— We have had rain, constant almost, for 3 days— I have quantities of things to write, but Bubba[173] is not very well—& so will be obliged to post pone till another time— He has an attack of Dysentery—which has come on so suddenly, that I really feel [illegible]— But if he is not better, in the morning, will send for a Homeopath.[174] of whom I have heard

---

[173] Bubba is the nickname of Bessie and Barrington's youngest son.
[174] Homeopathic doctor.

much— His cheeks are crimson, & he tosses from side to side & breaths very loud. he has no symptoms of cold—at all.

I am sorry Eva[175] mentioned my fall at Atlanta to you- it really made me almost ill in Augusta— But I did not tell you in my note, *simply* because I knew it would trouble you- I am quite well, so far is my *back* is concerned—& really feel better every way, & keep quite cool. not withstanding the Yankees— Genl. Stuart was buried this afternoon—poor fellow! Kiss my precious Boy for me, you are *right* not to let him learn too fast, in his book— *Oral* instruction, I think never harmed any one, and am quite willing that *you* should decide *when* to stop him- Precious baby, I long to hold him in my arms, once more. B— [Bubba] has a great tale, which he tells me every morning, regularly, but you mustnt let any body hear this, He says, with a wise look, "Bubba pea his *drawers* Mama:" & as solemnly, as he used to say "Good morning" to you

Love to dear Father, Marie[176] & Florrie[177]—&

with a heart full , & many thanks

for your care of Hadder[178]

I remain your Aff Bessie

When the fighting was fierce and time that could be devoted to writing was limited, King sent telegraphs in order to let his family know he was safe. The following telegraph is the one mentioned in the previous letter, which Bessie enclosed with her letter to his parents. It is missing several fragments.

---

[175] Catherine Evelyn "Eva" King Baker was the sister of Barrington S. King.

[176] Marie was Mary Reid Clemons, the widow of Thomas Edward King.

[177] Florrie was Florence Stilwell of New York, wife of Ralph Brown King.

[178] Harris was the oldest son of Barrington S. and Bessie.

THE SOUTHERN TELEGRAPH COMPANIES
Richmond May 11 1864

Care Rev C.H. Read[179]

Two [illegible] days of hard fighting and [illegible] yet safe thank god our army continues victorious Every Engagement

BS King
Lt Col

As pressure mounted toward Atlanta, James Roswell King, commander of the troops in Roswell, was faced with the Union Army coming through his hometown, set on destroying the factories his family had built. Adjutant A. W. Harris wrote to James on behalf of Colonel Wright, emphasizing his role in preventing surprise in Roswell, and in turn, in Atlanta. Wright was particularly concerned about the artillery King's troops possessed, fearing they would fall into the hands of the enemy. To stress this point, Wright wrote that "No apprehension of trouble is felt from any other than raiding parties (cavalry), and they would not, likely, bring artillery with them, and should they get possession of yours, it would enable them greatly to damage us here."[180] In the case that King's small group of troops were unable to control the Union forces, they were to fall back across the river and burn the bridge.

---

[179] Rev. or Dr. C. H. Read, with whom Bessie was staying with during spring 1864.

[180] OR, ser. 1, vol. 38, pt. 4, p. 727.

Richmond May 29th 1864
My Darling Mother,
    A very long time has passed since I wrote to any of you at home. This is the first opportunity I have had since the campaign began. I hope Bessie has written you for although unable to write to her, have telligraphed her frequently. I know you must have been very uneasy about me, for this has been a terrible campaign scarcely a day without a hard fight or heavy skirmishing. My health has been excellent though it all until Thursday last a half hour after I had written to Bessie telling her how well I was I was suddenly attacked with Dysentery & sent yesterday to the Hospital in this place where I am now writing you. I am better to day & dont think there is any danger having had no fever. I telligraphed Bessie at Staunton [Virginia,] yesterday to come to me But am sorry I did not as I expect to be back with my Regt in 2 two or three days & she will have the long trip by way of Lynchburg to get here. The Yankees have torn up about 20 miles of the R.R. [railroad] to Staunton. When I left the front Friday morning the enemy were moving down the Pamunky[181] it is presumed to occupy the same ground that McClelland[182] did in 1862 nearly 2 years ago. You have seen every thing in the papers how we have whipped them in every fight & that now Grant[183] cant get his men to attack us & has by flanking us gradually worked his way down nearly to Richmond I

---

[181] Pamunky River northeast of Richmond VA.

[182] Gen. George Brinton McClelland, U.S., was given command of the armies around Washington, DC. He was a natural at the complex task of organizing and training soldiers but lacked the necessary qualities needed to command large forces in battle. Most notably, the administration grew tired of his reluctance to march against the enemy. After Antietam, he delayed in pursuing Gen. Robert E. Lee, CSA, forcing President Abraham Lincoln to replace him with Gen. Ambrose E. Burnside (Boatner, *Civil War Dictionary*, 524).

[183] Gen. Ulysses Simpson Grant, U.S.

don't think there will be much fighting before the last of this week when I hope to be in at the big fight. As far as human eyes can see or knowledge extend Grant will be the worse whipped Gen that has ever tried to take Richmond. We have the largest and the best army that has ever been collected in the Confederacy & if so peace God we can not be whipped.

I have been very uneasy about you precious Mother & all at home hearing that Johnson[184] was falling back & believing he would go back across the Chattahoochee[185] But yesterdays paper says he has come back as far as he intends, which I sincerely hope is so & that our home will be safe. Dr. Reid[186] came to see me as soon as he heard I was here. Mrs Reid will come to day He asked me to go to their house but as neither my wife or svt [servant] is here & this disease is so troublesome I wont go up until my wife comes. Uncle Stiles[187] is here but I have not seen him Saw Rob, Randy & Eugene[188] Monday last at Hanover Junction.[189] They were all well. Aunt Cliff[190] was at Gordonsville.[191] I have not heard a word from Bessie in 12 days.

---

[184] Gen. Joseph E. Johnston, CSA.

[185] Chattahoochee River, north of Atlanta GA and south of Roswell GA.

[186] It appears that Dr. Reid is the same Rev. C. H. Read with whom Bessie stayed in the spring.

[187] Joseph Clay Styles (sometimes "Stiles") was the husband of Caroline Clifford "Aunt Cliff" Nephew, the half sister of Catherine Margaret Nephew, Barrington S. King's mother.

[188] Robert Augustus Stiles, Randolph Railey Stiles, and Eugene West Stiles were sons of Joseph Clay Styles.

[189] Hanover Junction is north of Hanover Courthouse VA and is the junction of the Virginia Central Railroad and the Richmond and Potomac Railroad.

[190] Caroline Clifford Nephew was the wife of Joseph Clay Styles.

[191] Gordonsville is south of Orange Courthouse VA.

But hope she will be here in the morning. Mr. Pleasants has had varioloid[192] badly & have not seen him.

The great & terrible fight of the war is yet to take place. God our Father had been merciful to me & to me in preserving my life through all thus far. Our army has not lost very heavy yet. My Regt has had 1 Capt killed 1 Lieut mortally wounded & 15 privates wounded. I do most earnestly pray God to give us the victory in this great struggle & let peace be restored to our country once more. May He bless you my dear Mother & spare us all the meet when this war shall end pray.

Your loving son,
B.S. King

Richmond May 30/64

Rev W E Baker[193]

Is Mrs King [Bessie] with you has she left for this place & by what Route I am Better if she is with you tell her to remain answer Home

Lt Col B.S. King

The following letter gives King's impression of the Confederate forces engagement at Trevilian Station, which took place on 11 June 1864. At this time, Cobb's Legion consisted of ten companies and was part of Young's Brigade with Lieutenant General Wade Hampton leading the Confederate Cavalry Corps. The Confederate forces engaged at Trevilian Station, 11 June 1864, is broken down as follows:

---

[192] Varioloid is a mild form of variola, or smallpox, occurring in a person who has had a previous attack or who has been vaccinated.

[193] Rev. William E. Baker was the husband of Catherine Evelyn "Eva" King, Barrington S. King's sister.

Confederate Cavalry Corps Lieut. General Wade Hampton

Butler's Brigade Major General M.C. Butler
4th S.C.
5th S.C.
6th S.C.

Rosser's Brigade
7th Va.
11th Va.
12th Va.
White's battalion (two companies)

Young's Brigade
Cobb's Legion (10 companies)
Phillip's Legion (six companies)
Jeff Davis Legion (four companies)
7th Ga. Cav. (ten companies)
Millen's Ga. Battalion (four companies)

Lee's Division Major General Fitzhugh Lee

Wickham's Brigade
1st Va.
2nd Va.
3rd Va.
4th Va.

Lomax's Brigade
5th Va.
6th Va.
15th Va.

Horse Artillery
Hart's (S.C.) Battery
Thomson's (Va.) Battery
Va. Battery

Total Confederate forces 5,000

There were a total of thirteen regiments and three battalions engaged in the battle.[194]

Staunton Va. June 14th 1864

My Darling Mother

I am as you will see at Staunton receiving a slight wound on last Saturday in our big cavalry fight at Trevillian[195] (near Gordonsville) an account of which you have probably seen in the papers. I recd the wound during a charge from some of the blue rascals[196] who had dismounted in the woods on the left of the road down which we were pursuing the running cowards as fast as our horses could go. As we passed, these fellows dismounted on the left of the road, they fired a volley into us and a ball grazed my right shoulder making a sore little wound a half inch wide &

---

[194] *Civil War On Line Order of Battle*, 2001 <http://web2.iadw.net/mbusby/strevlan.htm> (12 May 2003).

[195] Trevilian Raid took place 7–28 June 1864. The raid began when Grant abandoned operations around Cold Harbor and crossed the James River to attack Petersburg VA. Grant ordered Sheridan to cause a diversion with his cavalry forces. Sheridan was to join forces with Hunter and attack the Virginia Central Railroad. Lee learned of Sheridan's movements and ordered Wade Hampton and Fitz Lee, along with cavalry, to stop the destruction of the line. Custer's brigade stopped Lee's advancing column, passing between the two Confederate forces and capturing Hampton's horse and supply wagons. Hampton was able to turn quickly and recapture his supplies and his horses, as well as to capture several hundred Federal troops and Custer's headquarters wagon (Boatner, *Civil War Dictionary*, 848).

[196] Union forces wore blue uniforms.

two inches long.[197] I was sent to Charlottesville[198] but my wife being up here I came right up as the Yanks had all left. Bessie will tell you all about them. I cant write any more now my darling Mother as it is my right shoulder & I feel badly having had headache all day. I have written you frequently & hope you have recd them always once often twice a week. We feel very uneasy about our home But trust that the same kind heavenly Father who has mercifully spared my life through so many dangers will be merciful to you my dear parents & permit us yet to meet in peace & safety in our old house & home. With much love to dear father & yourself my darling Mother with kisses for Harris, I am

Your loving son,
B.S. King

The following letter was an appendage to the previous letter.

My Dearest Mother its has been such a long time since I wrote you, & now I will finish Barringtons letter, as his arm pains him too much to write more. He has Diarrhea, which I feel troubled about. I do not know, whether you have heard of his having been sick in the Hospital in Richmond with Dysentery. It was impossible for me to go to him, being ill myself. & now he has been in hard service, and looks most wretchedly thin & worn. I *feared* a relapse, & now he has a *fever*, which was very great last night, but only *slight* for an hour or so, today. He looks better though to night; & I trust he may soon recover.

---

[197] In his report on the battle, Maj. Gen. Wade Hampton, commanding 1st Division, Cavalry Corps, gave a detailed account of the fighting. His division took 570 prisoners in addition to the Federal wounded, while 59 of his troops were killed, 258 wounded, and 295 missing. Lt. Col. King was among the wounded he mentioned by name (*OR,* ser. 1, vol. 36, pt. 1, p. 1096).

[198] Charlottesville is between Staunton and Gordonsville along the railroad.

The wound which B. calls a "little scratch," is about an *inch* wide and two long. I dressed it and could see. it has been very painful all day. I had a terrible fright today. Groyson, Evelines husband, who is devoted to B— ran in, saying the Yankees were coming.- Mr. Harper, loaned him *his* horse and sick as he was, off he started.— I got terribly excited, about it, knowing how *sick* he *was*. but he went down, the street, & found it all *false*. I have not gotten over it yet,—but believe I could not stand a second dose of the Yankees, so well as the first. We all feel so thankful *you* did not stay at home to face them. Dear little Harris, how I have missed him, its has made me wretchedly homesick and blue. Then again, when the Yankees came here, I was *glad* that he was with you. But I have thought sometimes that he must have been very much in the way, amidst all you troubles at dear old Roswell. We scarcely even hope that R. [Roswell, Georgia] has escaped the vile yankee torch. Dear Mother; we are now at a station just beyond the Tunnel, a place called Greenwood—where we will stay, until all aprehension of the enemy returning to Staunton, has passed. B— was so nervous- & unwell, that we all thought best, for him to be in a quiet place. He looks so thin & haggard, it distresses me very much. But he has less Diarrhea today, & I trust will soon be improved.

The following letter is from Bessie to Mrs. Catherine M. King, Barrington's mother. While near the front with Barrington, Bessie wrote to his parents frequently regarding Barrington's health and their well-being. Many of the letters she and Barrington wrote were either delayed in the mail or were lost. Much of this letter expresses their desire to keep the family informed.

Staunton July 6th 1864

My Dearest Mother,

I have just heard from B-[199] in Richmond, that Bro. Jim[200] had Telegraphed Dr. Read,[201] for information of his welfare (Barringtons). I suppose you will *get this*, as we will send by Express— You *cant* think my precious Mother how badly I feel, at your not hearing of his movements. As I mentioned in *previous* letters, B. has written to *you*, even *since* I came once *at least* every week & *most of the* time *twice*— While in Richmond, I wrote *once* a week, as I have done *ever since I left you*, & sent *you* <u>8</u> *telegrams*—during the *early* part of the Campaign— We feel *grieved* about your not hearing from *one* or *both* of us- & sincerely hope you did not set it down to neglect of what was at *once* a *duty* & *a pleasure*. While sick, after coming here, & then cut, off from communicating with you, I lost the number of my letters, and all this time together, took about <u>4</u> *weeks* & consequently <u>4</u> letters from my correspondence. But with this exception, I have never *failed* to write *to you*.

Barrington was very ill in the Hospital at Richmond, with Dysentery—& I was too ill to sit up, run, here, at the time—— First of June, on 3d, he returned to Camp— on the 12th at "Trevillism," [Trevilian, Virginia] Hamptons Cavalry fight with Sheridan,[202] he received a flesh wound in the *right shoulder* & came up to Staunton on Monday— he went off refugeeing, for a week, & then he came back & spent a week *here* leaving on Wednesday a week ago for Camp— *All* of this, we have written you, in different letters, giving *full* details, & only *hope* you will have received them ere this—

---

[199] Barrington S. King.

[200] James Roswell King was a brother of Barrington S. King.

[201] Rev. C. H. Read, with whom Bessie stayed earlier in the year.

[202] Philip Henry Sheridan "Little Phil" was appointed colonel 25 May 1862 of the 2d Cavalry Brigade, Federal forces. His Trevilian Raid, 7–28 June 1864, was blocked by Wade Hampton (Boatner, *Civil War Dictionary,* 747).

Poor Barrington, he has *so few* people outside of the family who he cares particularly for, and *now* "*the friend*" of *his love*, next to our lamented Col. Delany,[203] poor *Frank Jones*,[204] he finds was killed during his absence— He told Barrington, *that* he expected to be killed in the *very* first *fight*, & die *instantly*—well, he passed through the first, but the second Hampton had with Sheridan, he *was killed, instantly!*

I feel so much sympathy for B- Ever since July 6th- they have slept together, invariably, & always messed [ate] together, B— spoke of him constantly while at Home. the report that Col. Weight[205] was to be made a Brig. Genl. troubled him, because Frank [Frank Jones] being Adjutant, of Cobb Legion & so good an one, *he knew* Col. W. would take him— Poor fellow, there will be *no* trouble on *that* point *now*. B. feels this blow bitterly, & if it was me, I think I should *want* no more intimate friends, in the army. They, with the Chaplain, had *just* formed a separate mess [dining together]. The Chaplain, was captured, the day B. was wounded & now Frank gone, no *one* is left with B. poor fellow it is so sad—

We have all written you repeatedly about the Yankees here & their conduct— I pray daily I may *never* be with them again— Oh! it was horrible past *all* descriptions! Dear Mother it is so hard on you & father, to be driven away from your sweet home, & to leave it all the dear old church, the graves of your loved children, & *all that* is so hard & grievous— We have heard nothing later than 31st of May from you- & have been very much worried by a rumor, that the factory has been burned— B. did not from *the first* believe it—& Mr. B. [Baker] does not now— Thought I am *still* afraid— Dear little Harris[206], I do so

[203] William G. Delony, Cobb's Legion, Company C.

[204] Frank Jones, Cobb's Legion, first lieutenant adjutant.

[205] G. Weigle, Georgia 7th Cavalry, Company A.

[206] Harris was the oldest son of Bessie and Barrington.

long to hear of him, & *all* about how he is, if he is good, though with *you* management, I feel pretty easy on that point. But *still* he is my *big boy,* & sadly do I miss him.

B. has sent me a *very good* ambrotype of himself & says he has some card Photographs to come this week, one for you & one for Eva.[207] I dont *much* think they will be good from what he says. Bubba[208] sends you sweet kisses.

The following letter is from Barrington to his mother.

Petersburg[209] July 7th 1864

My Darling Mother,

I have opportunity to sending a letter through to Geo by a gentleman going to Athens & avail myself of it by writing, as I expect my letters have been a long time in reaching you, & many of them have not nor ever will judging from what the mail is here.

I left Staunton a week ago yesterday my wound well enough to return to my command, & it seems impossible to get to it. Jessy[210] will probably be in to day though with my horse and by tomorrow hope ever more to be in duty. The Regt is stationed about 25 miles from here on the Petersburg & Welden R.R. [railroad] to protect the Road from raids the last one having torn up all the RRs leading south and for the time being cut us off from communication by Rail. You have seen in the papers what

---

[207] Catherine Evelyn "Eva" King Baker was the sister of Barrington S. King.

[208] Bubba is the nickname of Barrington, the second child of Bessie and Barrington.

[209] Petersburg VA is due south of Richmond, and a rail line connects the two.

[210] Jessy was a slave, referred to as a servant by the Kings, who followed Barrington S. King and assisted him.

the Raiders have done & what we have done to them. Every thing is quiet since then except Infantry skirmishing along our lines with an occassional shell into the city of Petersburg. It is distressing to see & to know the amount of terrible suffering caused by this useless & wicked bombardment of a place which if burst to the ground would not bring the Yankees one inch nearer to the city or to Richmond. The whole city with the exception of a house here & there is entirely deserted & to walk the silent Streets the foot fall echoes drearily from the houses more or less riddled by the shell which every few minutes come tearing & plunging through. The Hotel "Garratts" [identity unknown] is still kept open for the accommodation of the public while sitting in the piazzo[211] day before yesterday 3 shell of the "lamp post" order burst in the yard of the foundry just opposition, The Yankee aim being attracted by the smoke, sent those as a "gentle" hint that no work was to be done in the city of that kind. The hands (mostly negroes) came out at the first explosion like hornets when their nest is stirred up, but unlike hornets did not wait to defend but struck a "Bee" line for a safer place.

The Hotel is thus far safe in fact most of the shelling has been confined to that part of town near the Appomatox River. The citizens are camping in the suburbs & woods around the city old men women & children. I heard through a Major Johnston[212] from Roswell up to the 27th of June at which time Roswell he said was safe. I am very anxious to hear from him it has been a long time since I have had the pleasure. Bessie Eva & all were quite well & have written often to you. I hope you get their letters. Kiss dear little Hadder for me. With a sons best love to dear father & yourself & earnest prayers that we may meet in safety & health in His own good time

---

[211] Piazza is a large, covered porch.

[212] Possibly George Doherty Johnston, of 25th Alabama.

I am very aftly your loving son

B.S. King

In early July 1864, 11th Company of Cobb's Legion was assigned to Phillip's Legion Cavalry under Captain F. E. Eve, and the first ten companies of Cobb's Legion, cavalry, constituted the 9th Regiment Georgia Cavalry, to the command of which Colonel G. J. Wright was hereby assigned.

During summer 1864 the tone of the letters changes, demonstrating the anxiety the King family felt as the means of communications were cut and news of fighting in north Georgia caused them a great deal of concern. In addition, the lack of supplies needed by both the army and the civilians becomes more obvious. Everyone feels the panic. The letters become quicker paced in their language and the question as to whether prior letters have been received causes numerous repeats. Added to the confusion and desire for materials is the new baby expected in mid-October.

Camp near Stony Creek Depôt

July 14th 1864

My Dear Father

Your letter of the 14th last was recd two days since. Was glad to hear from you even of date so long since, the last we heard being of 27th May. I am very anxious to hear of late dates from home. We have had no southern mail at all for over 3 weeks, ever since the Raid on the Danville R.Rd. [railroad] I was very glad indeed to hear through one of the Phillips Legion who left Atlanta ~~yesterday~~ last Friday that Johnston keeps a force on north side of the river to protect the bridges & the Factory &

that the Factory is yet safe. I hope it can be protected until Johnston forces Sherman to retreat, but feel fearful that he will continue to fall back to draw Sherman still further from his base of supplies. I am afraid if it is destroyed the effect on your health we [would] be bad, as it will leave you no employment for your mind, which has for so many years been so actively employed, that having nothing to do you will feel it very much. And then if you move to Savh [Savannah, Georgia] at this season of the year, Mother and yourself will miss the [illegible]acing climate of upper Georgia so much it may make you both sick. Savh is so debilitating especially at this season of the year. Every thing is in the hands of an omnipotent God who will do those things best for our own good & His Glory.

I confess I dont like the idea of Dr Geigers[213] keeping my share of profits & spending it, I am not at all willing to enter into *any more speculations* or *business* of *any* kind with *him*. He knows nothing more of business than a child & the delusive prospects of making millions out of his first speculation has completely turned his mind. Please Father tell him for me my expenses are so great & not wishing to use any more of the proceeds of my wifes stock in the Factory which I desire to accumulate for my wife & children, not knowing what my [may] happen. And I wish to support my family hereafter on what my portion of the card machines can make me. To do this it is necessary for me to have my portion of all monies made by it or the wire paid as promptly as possible. I am now in need of funds & would like a draft for the amnt sale of wire and all my share of proceeds card machines, sent to you that I may through Kent Paine & Co draw on you for what I may wish. If you think it advisable I am willing to sell out every thing wire & machines & get rid of it entirely. If I was at Macon to stay, could make a good thing of it, but am afraid of Dr Geiger, his brain is decidedly

---

[213] Charles A. Geiger's.

affected with a "money mania" which unless he is watched will sink all my profits & his own. Please Father attend to it for me, I can no do any thing for myself here in the army.

We have good news now, our "large force" is doing wonders in Maryland & Penna & before two weeks the whole of both armies will be two hundred miles from Richmond. Grant can do nothing with noble old Lee. I wish Johnston could get rid of Sherman in the same way. Kiss Hadder for me. Give much love to dear Mother, & may God bless you both with strength to bear all trials He may see fit to inflict, sparing our lives to meet when this war shall end, earnestly prays

Your Affectionate Son, B.S. King

The following letter was written by Barrington to his mother during the Battle of Atlanta.

Camp near Stony Creek Depot

July 20th 1864

My Dearest Mother

I am feeling very uneasy about Father & yourself & little Haddie. It has been so long since I have heard from you & the date of the letter was the 14th of June. & now the Danville R Rd [railroad] is finished & mails have come through & yet I can hear nothing from yourself or Father. Members of the Regt lately from Atlanta returning to duty bring such conflicting rumors too that I feel doubly anxious to hear. One man says they have not only destroyed the factories but that most of the buildings in the village[214] has been burnt. Another says they have only burnt the Wool Mill & are running the Cotton Mill on their own account & have burnt more of the buildings in the village. Another one says the factory was burnt under the British flag. I don't know

---

[214] Roswell GA is the village to which he is referring.

what to believe but know this that if it is not already burnt it will
if Sherman is ever forced to retreat be destroyed without a doubt.
It was reported too that Johnston had decided to give up Atlanta
But now he has been superceded by "hood"[215] who will fight
Sherman where he is. All Bessies letters to me show the great
anxiety She & Eva[216] feels about you. I don't think father &
yourself ought to venture to Savh [Savannah, Georgia] at this
season of the year. I am afraid Father particulary will suffer from
it having nothing to occupy mind or body & I don't believe he
could exist in the healthiest place without having a plenty of
business on hand all the time.

It will be hard to have to give up our old home with which
every year of my life for many years in full of such pleasant
associations all of us your children & grand children will feel it.
But what will your feelings be my dear Mother. God give you
grace to bear all the trials & sorrows he may see fit to inflict.

I met Joseph Simmons of the Roswell Guards Co (H) 7th
Geo Regt in Petersburg the other day & he gave me ($50) Fifty
dollars to ask Bro Jim[217] to pay it to his wife. she worked in his
Mill. Will you please ask Bro Jim to pay it to her & charge the
same to me.

---

[215] Gen. John B. Hood, CSA, was commissioned 1st lieutenant in 1861
and was sent to command Magruder's cavalry force. He was appointed brigadier
general 6 March 1862. After Gaines' Mill, Second Bull Run, and Antietam, he
was promoted to major general 10 October 1862. He was severely wounded in
the left arm at Gettysburg and recovered to participate in Chickamauga, where
he lost his right leg. He was promoted to lieutenant general on 1 February
1864. He replaced Gen. Joseph E. Johnston on 17 July 1864, just before the
Battle of Atlanta. He kept the title of general temporarily after the replacement
(Boatner, *Civil War Dictionary,* 407–408).

[216] Catherine Evelyn "Eva" King Baker was the sister of Barrington S.
King with whom Bessie was staying.

[217] James Roswell King was a brother of Barrington S. King.

I have told you about our having a Chaplain for our Regt a friend of Frank Jones who was the best friend I had in the Regt. Mr Cooper our Chaplain is a graduate of seminary at Columbia a very worthy young man and having been a private in the service ever since the war until his appointment of Chaplain to our Regt is not afraid of explosion & works hard & faithfully with the Regt We have prayer meeting every evening a little after sun set which is well attended & much good is already seen as the result many are anxious & many inquiring besides stirring up the members of churches. For some weeks past my dear mother since about the 1st of June I have been in a very happy frame of mind. My faith having increased, and my love increasing with my faith I thank my God, His Holy Spirit has given me fresh & greater strength & has enabled me to lay all my burdens at the foot of the cross I need yet greater faith & more strength for the performance of my duties and I continually pray to my heavenly Father that my heart may be full. I partook of the Lords supper while in Richmond for the first time in 18 months it being the only opportunity I have had for so long. I feel that the blood of our crucified Lord & saviour has been made precious to my soul & that through him my salvation is sure. I know myself to be weak & that I fall far short in the performance of all my duties yet that does not prevent my going to god through the merits of Jesus Christ who died that such sinners as myself might be saved. God grant this feeling I have may be true repentance & Godly sorrow for my sins & that there is no self righteousness or vain glory may be in my heart.

Kiss my dear Haddie I would like so much to see him May God bless you both my dear Parents & give you strength for your days of trial & spare our lives that we may meet on earth in due season earnestly prays your own loving Son

B.S. King

The following letter, which totals four pages in the original form, is faint due to having been written with weak ink. This letter was written just days after the Battle of Atlanta and indicates the desire of soldiers to hear from home regarding the destruction of the city.

Camped Near Stoney Creek Depôt   July 25th, 1864

My darling Mother,

Nearly six weeks have passed since the date of my last letter from Father. I am getting very uneasy & exceeding anxious to hear how and when Father, yourself, Harris & all of Roswell are. Major Minturn tells me he hears regularly from his wife. It was through her we have heard of the destruction of our little village. The factory & every home in the place being burnt. It is impossible for me to realize it, and I want to hear all about it from some of the family. Where are Ralph[218] and Bro. Jim?[219] Facing the enemy I hope. Oh how fiercely I could fight to drive the scandals from my home that their presence might no longer pollute my native state. In all my engagements with the enemy when I come in sight of their blue yankee uniforms a feeling more like that of a fiend than human takes possession of me and I only feel an intense desire to kill, to strike to the earth all that come in my reach. "Vengeance is mine I will repay thus saith the Lord." That this will not make it sinful for me to feel even a stronger desire to use my upmost soul felt desire to drive them from the soil they now pollute, & to recover the homes they have made desolate, yes that they have utterly destroyed until thousands are now homeless. I suppose you have all gone to Savh [Savannah, Georgia] since the enemy crossed the [Chattahoochee] river. I rejoice that Johnston has been

---

[218] Ralph Brown King was a brother of Barrington S. King.

[219] Jim was James Roswell King, another brother of Barrington S. King.

superceded by Hood. We have heard of the fighting there & are anxiously looking for further news. Atlanta, I expect, it now safe & I pray God we may have such audictory then as will have to an early termination or cessation of hostilities but what will Father and yourself do for a home. Dear old Roswell I am afraid we never will meet in a home there again. Oh what a war, a cruel war, & how little the yankees feel it.

I hear from Bessie regularly. Eva & herself are quite well. Bessie had a tremendous scare the other day from a cow that had got its horns fastened in a gate & wrenching one off it took after her in its agony and came very near catching her. She feels no bad effect from it though she tells me. She will be confined about the middle of October[220] and will again require several things for herself and child from [illegible] her baggage in Atlanta. I intend sending Jessy[221] to you that he may bring back everything she wishes a list of which will be furnished. I will send him soon as I hear that Atlanta is safe. She will require a nurse too as Martha[222] is not fit to take charge of an infant. I wrote both Father and yourself and hoped either Brother Charles[223] or Mr. Gignilliat[224] who I wrote to requiring them to try to find an expensive nurse for me have find one but if they have Claras[225] no good. She have a [illegible] Jessy bringing her own with him don't say anything to Clara about it. Only please when [illegible] comes for her to leave make her have take up sick or will blind & Jessy will take care of her to Stanton. Martha I will have sold unless I can dispose of her in a safe way that will cost me nothing. Bessie must have a good, careful nurse so that her health may not suffer

---

[220] She was expecting a baby due in mid-October.

[221] Slave that accompanied Barrington S. King during the war.

[222] Slave that accompanied Bessie to Virginia.

[223] Charles Barrington King was a brother of Barrington S. King.

[224] "Gignilliat" was Barrington's grandmother's maiden name; this was likely a relative.

[225] Slave of Barrington S. and Bessie King.

as it did after Barrington[226] was born & I lay all the troubles she
has had for so long to the fact of her having no nurse at the
time. But for this miserable, terrible war & I would trouble not
one to attend to anything for me but my hands are tied now and
all I can do is for my country, alone to fight & toil and suffer for
my country. Someone else must take care of my wife and my
interest. Father and yourself, my darling Mother, have done all
for me that a parent could do and I fully appreciate all your
kindness & parental love. But you both have troubles & trails too
many & hard to be having for me to trouble you any more now.

You will have seen before this reaches you that U. S. Grant
is certainly dead. We have had rumors of it several days but only
know it to be a fact today. It will have a very demoralizing effect
upon the army & the whole yankee nation. Meade, his successor,
is a very cautious & almost a timid man & already the siege of
Richmond and Petersburg has been wasted and both armies are
crossing the river as rapidly as possible. We may move at any
moment. I don't think Genl. Lee will go into Pennsl.
[Pennsylvania] this year if he does not the campaign for this
year is partially ended for the yankees so not the force [illegible]
dare attack us I [illegible] believe we will have peace for many
months yet but believe [illegible] this worst of this when is over
& most of the fighting a predatory guerilla kindly regiment
[illegible] the Calvary on both sides. God grant we may have a
cessation of hostilities which will lead an early peace.

I have told you about our Chaplain. We have had a prayer
meeting in our Regt. every evening for some weeks past. I have
been praying for strength in faith that I might take an active
part in them but always felt any old fear & diffidence that I
would break down & rest be able to speak a word or prayer to my
heavenly father before an audience. Last week our Chaplain had
to go to Richmond to get [illegible] hymns books & c. [etc.] for

---

[226] Barrington was the second child of Barrington S. and Bessie King.

the Regt. The first day I struggled all day against the feeling I knew to be my plain duty of conducting the meeting myself g____ing [illegible] my conscience with the old [illegible] of my heart beating as fast I would not be able to speak. The second night came and one of the men came to me to ask if the meeting could not go on. I told him it could and I would conduct it. I prayed earnestly to God for strength & my prayer was answered and though my effort was feeble, God seemed to have blessed it for the three meetings I conducted were attended by between three and four hundred of my Regt. & the interest seems to have increased & if we could only have a quite of a few weeks longer I would get Uncle Stiles [Reverend J. C. Styles] to preach for us. There are many who are amateurs and behold [illegible] up the Regt. how improved wonderfully in the last three weeks. God grant I earnestly pray we may [illegible] a glorious revival here & in authorizing of his Holy [illegible] which such [illegible] many [illegible] into the [illegible] of safety. Oh that we could have this outpouring of the Holy Spirit throughout our whole army, & our whole country so that we could as a nation praise God and He would bless us with an honorable and a lasting peace.

Kiss my dear little Hadder for me. Give much love to dear Father and love to all I pray God we may yet meet in health and safety when this war shall end.

Your loving son,

B. S. King

Staunton August 2d 1864-

My own precious Mother,

I write to send by Jessy, as Barrington will send him home; & I know it will reach you much *earlier* in this way. We have heard so little of your movements, that we *all* feel anxious to hear from dear Father or yourself, & *then* we will know certainly.

As it is, we hear rumors, which we cannot always rely on. but of course they make their own impression. I expected they would burn dear *beautiful* Roswell, that precious Home which we all loved. *I* love it, because both my little ones were born there, & so much of my married life has been passed there. But alas! from *all* we can learn, it must be a *perfect desolation*. Maj Minton[227] told B. that they had cut down every *shade* tree, after burning the homes of *all*. I feel more sad, for your being burned out of your Home, & such a *dear* precious home than any thing else. It is very hard, this destruction of property, but hardest of, all is the destruction of the villiage & particularly does this fall on *you* & father, having gone there & reclaimed it from the wilderness. But so it was ordered, that *all* shall suffer from Yankee invasion, all feel the iron heel of despotion. till not *one* yearning shall be left for the "Old Union"— It was no trial to me to give it up, & I am thankful. Barrington feels very much the destruction of his loved home. & has pledged himself to *retaliate* if he has the opportunity—

If Clara[228] has not been sold, we want Jessy to bring her on. She is, if good for *any* earthly thing, able to nurse, at least for 3- or 4 months. Before that time B— will try to make some sort of arrangement for me as I have *no place now* to call home & some thing I *must* have, poor as it may be. He will arrange it all, if he is spared & try to find *some* spot away from the Yankees. It would be impossible for me to be running about from one place to another, with a little infant,[229] provided we had the means. But not to be thought of, under present circumstances.

---

[227] Maj. John Minton, who fought with Gen. Andrew Jackson and Davy Crockett on the frontier. He moved to Roswell in 1849 and served in the Civil War. He was injured in the first battle.

[228] Slave who stayed with Bessie and Barrington in Virginia.

[229] Catherine Margaret, nicknamed Maggie, is the infant with whom Bessie was pregnant at the time.

I feel so nervous this morning I can not write legibly—the weather is *so* very hot & debilitating. I do not know how you *all stand* it, so low down as Macon & Sav. [Savannah] my dear little baby Harris how *much* I long for him— I feel very badly about it too, your having him fearing he may have been much trouble, under *your* circumstances, & wish I had brought him with me for I *know* he must have been in the way. If the day shall *ever come,* that B. can come Home & we *have* a home it will be *more* than I expect. But I think of it *much* & long for it greatly. I hope Harris is well, bless his heart, we miss him *so much.*

Eva wants to keep Martha,[230] *why* I do not know. for she was *very much* afraid of having her here, while the Yankees were here. & would have sent her off, if possible— At all events, she will be *hired* out as soon as C[231]— comes—for she acts so badly I cant possibly keep her about me. And with her *hire* I can pay for my washing until I leave Va. Eva does not want her until 1st of Jan. & I hope to be settled down somewhere long before that time.

I hoped Jessy would be able to bring on my little things for me, but hear Atlanta will soon be given up, & nothing will be saved I fear. It will be a great loss to *me* for *all* I possess- though it is not much, will be *lost* & we cant afford to buy the little I need. for the little one. I dont see my way clearly, how B. is to support us, but try not to worry about it. sometimes it is impossible to prevent myself from feeling low spirited, but keep it off when possible—

I have written every week, until the last, & was expecting Jessy then, which prevented my doing so— Do ask Florrie[232] to write, if you do not feel like it dearest mother, for really I have

---

[230] Martha was a slave who had been with Bessie.

[231] Clara is the slave Bessie requested to be sent from Roswell.

[232] Florrie was Florence Stilwell of New York, wife of Ralph Brown King, thus Bessie's sister-in-law.

only had 2 letters from you since I left Home 4 *long* months ago— Long & sad they have been to me. But I feel so grateful for B's safety, that I cannot find it in my heart to say any thing has been hard upon us—

> Love to dear sisters & father
> and *very much* for your self. Your aff.
> Bessie

The following letter is from Barrington to his father.

Camp on Nottoway river August 5th 1864

My Dear Father

I have an opportunity of sending a letter by Mr Jones [unknown] direct to you & write again for fear you may not have recd my letters about business.

I want to break up my partnership with Dr Geiger[233] & believe it unsafe to be in business with as careless & stupid a man as he appears to be. I have been speaking with a lawyer in the Regt about it & small concern as it is, through Dr G- carelessness or dishonesty if he should prove so I might be involved to a large amount. At any rate I dont feel safe & as the concern has payed me nothing will willingly take my share of proceeds up to date & dispose of my proportion of value of wire & machines to any man who wishes to buy. Of course I want it to sell for as much as it can bring. I will leave it entirely to you though father to do what you can for me, for it is impossible for me to do anything of the kind or attend to any business matters now. Any way I want Dr Geiger to pay over my share of proceeds at once, so that I can support my wife from it & not be compelled to use any

---

[233] Charles Geiger.

more of the proceeds of the factory, now that the principal has been destroyed I want what it has made to accumulate so that when the war ends my wife may have some property of her own. The yarn you mentioned, 8 bales as being on hand for me, I would like to have kept in a safe place & not sold before winter at any rate my wife said she would like to have about 20 bunches saved to have clothing made for svts[234] and children. I would like very much to know how I stand & what property I have invested.

I expect to send Jessy to you father some time this month that he may bring on all the clothing & "fixings" my wife may require also to bring on *a nurse* for the baby.[235] I am willing to give every negro I have got to get *one good reliable nurse* for my wife, to save her all trouble of body & anxiety of mind when the child is born, as I said before I believe her months of sickness & pain were caused by her having no suitable nurse when Barrington was born. And now as I believe her health has entirely recovered, my greatest desire is to keep her well. Please father if a good nurse can be had, buy her for me at any price for Bessie *must* have a good one. I have just had a conversation with our Commissary "Mr. Few"[236] from Thomasville who says he knows of an excellent nurse belonging to his Brother inlaw & as he (Few) will leave for home next week on a sick furlongh he will write you about her. Jessy will take letters from Bessie telling Mother what she requires. If our things have been destroyed in Atlanta ask Mother please to buy all that would be necessary for the comfort of Bessie & her child. Every thing has remained quiet since the attempt of Grant to destroy us by springing a mine. His loss was so heavy & ours so small I doubt if he ever attempts it again.

---

[234] Servant is how the Kings referred to their slaves.

[235] Bessie's unborn child, Catherine Margaret, nicknamed Maggie.

[236] M. C. Few was commissary in Cobb's Legion.

Give much love to dear Mother. And a kiss for my little Hadder. Am glad you all were in Savh [Savannah] when that raid to Macon took place. & am very glad to see by the papers that all of those raids have been pretty well broken up. They do a great deal of harm to the country but *cant conquer* us but rather stirs us up to greater efforts to repel the rascals. In that way it will be of great service to upper Georgia where there were so many who *professed* Union sentiments which the Yankees do not respect at all. Eva & Bessie & all quite well when I heard from them last. May God bless you my dear parents & permit us to meet again in safety prays

Your Affectionate Son,
B.S. King

The date of the following letter is unknown, but it would have been written by Bessie to her mother-in-law during late summer or early fall 1864.

❖

Staunton

My dearest Mother,

I write this letter to go by Jessy on the first "horse detail"— I want to beg yourself or Florrie,[237] *if possible* to get out of my large box— 8- of my table cloths—& take the *little box*—which has the baby clothes in it & empty it into the black trunk of which I enclose the key. I want the *white* & *brown* shirting calico, night gowns & c [etc.]— You dont know how I *hate* to *worry you with* all this—dearest Mother, but I am *positively obliged* to have these things, for we cannot afford to buy *any of them*. Oh! my heart *sinks* within me— if it was not for my

---

[237] Florrie was Florence Stilwell of New York, wife of Ralph Brown King, thus Bessie's sister-in-law.

situation, I would not feel so depressed by it— But knowing as I
do, all the expense to be met—it *makes me* sad— Poor *dear old
Roswell*, we wait in fear & trembling *the end*, of all this
vandalism, & only heard this morning of the burning of the
Factory. I dont know *how* I feel, but *revengeful* I certainly
am—& would *burn* again— Maybe I am wrong, but it is my firm
conviction, that we *must retalliate*— Many Officers & men,
have made a solemn oath, not to leave *anything,* ~~when they go
into~~ if they go into the enemys country again—

Barrington goes again to the Army tomorrow, & I feel very
sad about it for now that a *Yankee bullet* has struck him— I
cannot feel, as heretofore, that *he* is safe. I shall almost certainly
expect, he will he wounded in the *next-fight*— How *terrible* it is
to think of *Roswell* being in ashes—as I fear it is.

B. does *not* believe its *true*, but Lieut Edward Clayton
[unknown] of Augusta took dinner here, & said he has read it, in
a Geo [Georgia] paper—

Dear Mother, I cannot write more now, but will write *by
mail*, as this may be months reaching you— I have an old white
Brillant, dress, in one of the trunks, which please send, as it may
do to make gowns—or frocks. And only think, I *believe* it will be
"Catherine Margaret"[238] this time— At any rate, I hope so—
One comfort, if she inherits *poverty* her Father will save a *name*
untarnished—& if *his life* is only spared, to see the end, *hard
work* will be no hardship—

I trust dear little Harris is well, oh! I do miss him so—&
when will I see him— dear boy, tell him Mamma thinks & talks
of him, every day, & we wish him with us— love to Father,
Florrie & *all* the dear ones— Give Hadder one of Grand mother's
[illegible] kisses for me tell I come home.

---

[238] Bessie thought the baby would be a little girl and had already picked
out the name Catherine Margaret.

Barrington joins me in *best* love to you, dearest mother & may God protect us all & let us meet in safety.

> Your Ever Affectionate,
> Bessie

> Camp Cobb Legion August 7th 1864

My Dearest Mother,

I will start Jessy off for Georgia tomorrow, but as he will have to take two of my horses down in the South western part of this state to be left there to recruit, he will be nearly two weeks in getting to Savannah. He will take with him two letters for you from Bessie. One was written some weeks ago when I left Staunton, & contains the key of her trunk containing certain articles she now requires. The other one I recd through the mail this morning also a letter for you from Aunt Cliff[239].

My Dear Mother, I know you can appreciate Bessies condition & my anxiety on her account. Please do what you can for her in getting the things wished for out of her trunk & boxes, & if they have been destroyed, please buy what she may wish, & have it paid for by Father. And then about the nurse. You know what a time of it Bessie had when Barrington was a baby in having no nurse. I am willing to let Jessy remain two or three weeks if by so doing he can bring on a capable nurse. I dont want him to return without one, for if he does I know my wife will have nothing but trouble both of body & mind, until she becomes an invalid again with all the pain & suffering of her old disease.[240]

---

[239] Caroline Clifford Nephew, half sister of Barrington S. King's mother.

[240] Probably childbirth, subsequent recovery, and the demands of caring for a newborn.

I am willing that a large price should be paid, & will consider it the best possible investment of money. Mr Few, our commosissary [commissary], has told me of one owned by his Brother in law in Thomas Co [Thomas County, Georgia] which if she can not be bought he is pretty sure, I could hire her for a year. But ask Father not to depend on that, but if a good one can be bought to buy her anyhow. It does seem very unfortunate for us that under the present circumstances a child should be given us to add additional care & expenses to what is already hard to be borne. But it is the dispinsation of providence, and as in ordinary times it would have been looked upon as a blessing from heaven, even so now we must consider it as such. I dont know what the poor little thing will do for clothing & c. [etc.] for it in impossible to buy, nor can we now afford it. Please my darling Mother do all you can to make both mother & child as comfortable as possible.

Every thing is quiet on the lines & no news that we can hear. We are now encamped on the Nottoway river some 14 miles below where we were on Stoney Creek. We take up an occasional deserter who always report great demoralization & c. but cant be depended on. It will not be long I expect before another raid on our Rail Roads is attempted by Sheridan.[241] We will have hot work when it does take place, but expect we are able to whip him whenver he attempts it. Old "Jubal"[242] is creating great excitement in Yankee dom. As yet they have burnt up but one town, Chambersburg. But if Cobb Legion gets up

---

[241] Philip Henry "Little Phil" Sheridan, U.S.

[242] Gen. Jubal Anderson "Old Jube" or "Jubilee" Early, CSA, was commissioned as colonel of 24th Virginia and was appointed brigadier general after commanding the regiment at First Bull Run. During the Peninsular campaign he was wounded. He was promoted to major general on 23 April 1863. After the Shenandoah Valley Campaign and the defeat at Waynesboro on 2 March 1865, he was relieved of duty due to pressures in public opinion (Boatner, *Civil War Dictionary*, 254–55).

there some others will in all probability be reduced to ashes. I hear Milledgeville has been burnt by the Yankee raiders. These raids give great suffering & reduce many to almost starvation but they can never subdue us by such fighting, in fact it will have the contrary effect upon us, & will make us more bitter, more determined than ever to never again counterance a Yankee or their nation. When every thing Bessie wishes, my dear Mother, has been collected, please send Jessy back with them to Staunton. Do dont let him come back without a nurse. Give a kiss to dear little Hadder. I hope he is a good boy. Give love to Father & all. May God bless you my darling Mother & spare our lives to meet in safety sincerely prays

Your loving son,
B.S. King

My Dear Mother, I recd a letter from Bessie yesterday that a tellegram from father stated he would probably come on to Staunton soon You will I sincerely hope come in too & bring our little boy. I think it would be the best thing Father & yourself could do to come on here until every thing quiets down in Georgia. I had made all preparations to send Jessy to you to day but Bessies letter has made me change my mind for if you come the things she requires might be brought on without giving me the expense. I send all the letters Jessy was to take home by mail also the letter with the key of the trunk I hope all will be safely recd. Hoping to see you & father & my dear little boy before long, I am,

Your loving son,
B.S. King

P.S. If you decide not to come on, I will send Jessy as soon as I hear.

The first four pages of this letter are missing; therefore, the date is unknown. It is from Bessie to Mrs. Catherine King written in late summer or early fall 1864.

Page 5

I wrote back to you & Florrie[243] last week, and fear you will feel *bored* by a repetition of things. But dear Mother, this is *for you to read* & no body else. I expect to be confined[244] about the 18th of *October*—& B. has promised to send Jessy home for what I *must* have. And when he goes, he will carry a key to my black trunk, which, please put the things in— *All* my baby clothes are in a small box—which *I hope* was saved— Please put them in the trunk— these is a lot of trash in it besides, but I want the white & brown shirting, the grey flannel for B's drawers. which he is *compelled* to have—my night gowns, the little things—& every piece of old flannel, that can be found in my boxes— then 3 table cloths out of *the big box*—& what ever else, *you* think would be useful—my little plain dresses, I had to replenish, & <u>5</u> little dresses, cost 300— of *course* I have no trimmings—just the *goods*. I only go 2 flannel petticoats at 25 pr. yd— There is some *calico* & an *old* brilliant dress, also, in the trunk which will be very useful—a lot of blue moreso scraps, in the top of the white trunk, & a bag with worsteds, & scrapes, in the *black* one. The worsted I want to knit little shoes, as I think of I will be obliged to put them on this winter— This *is my first* winter bird[245]—so am somewhat ignorant of *what* is necessary. I should *like* of all things, one of my little *pads* or cushions, as it is so impossible to get the raw cotton here to make one— poor

---

[243] Florrie was Florence Stilwell of New York, wife of Ralph Brown King, thus Bessie's sister-in-law.

[244] The baby was due.

[245] This was her first child born during the winter.

little ~~to~~ "Marsh Lacky" [unknown] *what a* wardrobe—it will possess—

Dear Mother, I am *so* sorry to give you all this worry & trouble. for indeed it troubles me, very much. & if I could *get* what I want, that is, *could afford* it would not send to you for them. But such things are not to be bought for money—& you *know* I could not at such rates, afford them, if they *could*— In my letter to *Florrie* [Florence Stillwell] last week, I begged her, if she could to save you this trouble—& put up the things for me— arrange this as you like—dear Mother, only dont worry your dear self with its at all my *more than* you can help—

In the present abominable mail system, we dont know whether you have even heard of poor Randys[246] wound. B. writes me, he was shot behind the *left* eye, the ball passing *out the nose*. He still suffers very much, but is walking about—& B. writes he thinks it *possible* he may recover the sight of his eye—poor fellow—we have not heard a word from Aunt Cliff, but *accidently* heard *one* of her Boys was wounded— *now* Barrington confirms it & we have only these particulars which I have written— I told you in my former letters that B. was quite ill when he came to me agrovated form of Diarrhea & scorching fevers— I will not say more of it now, hoping you may have received some of our letters, as we both wrote frequestly—& *would* have Telegraphed you of his wound, only, there was no Office here until a few days before he left-

For myself dear Mother, I *have* never in my life enjoyed more splendid health; I feel *well* & strong and *work hard* trying what I can do to get my poor little boy ready for Winter— He grows finely & is a *good* child, if I do say it—sprightly and bright as he can be. I *have never* been so perfectly well since my marriage, & *what* does it indicate? some dreadful *end?* or a Miss

---

[246] Randy was Randolph Railey Styles, a cousin of Barrington, the son of Aunt Cliff.

Catherine Margaret?[247] the latter I hope—for it would be *dreadful* to die now, while everything is so torn and distracted—& B. away from me. But I never *had* fewer fears & apprehensions in my life- dear precious little Harris, how I would love to have him here this evening. I think I miss him *more*, the longer I am absent from him. I hope he is well, & good. Kiss him for me & papa. We *often* wish we had him with us— we long more & more for a quiet home & peace in the land—oh! we all pray for it—& my God bestow it on us— May our Heavenly Father watch over & keep us, all, parents & children to meet in safety prays your aff. daughter

Bessy

Love to Father, Florrie, Sister Marie[248] & all—& a thousand kisses for Hadder, bless his precious life. Maurino [illegible] will write him a letter *next time*—& little Bubba[249] prays so earnestly for you all & *dear* Bubba Hadder.

The following is the last sheet of correspondence from Bessie to Mrs. Catherine King written in late summer or early fall 1864.

Page 5

The letter with the Key, has a hastily written list of what I required— I forgot to mention Grey flannel, which was in the Trunk. I want it exceedingly for Barringtons winter drawers— he will be obliged to have some this winter—as he has had no new ones—since the first winter of the war. I wrote to Florrie a long letter, but suppose she *did not* recieve it—as *I* have had no reply.

---

[247] Bessie felt well during this pregnancy and feared that her good health indicated something would go wrong with the birth. Catherine Margaret was the name she selected for the baby if it was a girl.

[248] Marie was the wife Thomas Edward King, a son of Barrington King's.

[249] Nickname of Barrington, Barrington and Bessie's second child.

I want the table cloths *more* ever than anything else. for there is no Diaper for sale. & of course it is indespensible[250]— It makes me feel blue to think being in such a condition in these awful times— But I try to be hopeful & cheerful, thinking it will *all* end well; & so I trust it may, for the sake of my husband & poor little Boys— They would have *only you*, in this world dear mother should I be taken from them.[251] Bubba is very sweet & grows fast. I think He is the greatest comfort to me— Cut off as I am from Barrington & my dear Little Harris- I know he will be glad to see Jessy, & do hope he is *well*, & a *good* boy. I *do hope* to have them all together in Dec- Barrington thinks he will be able to get off the, & go Home on *that* means to Georgia- I feel that we really *have* no home now. & sadly it makes me feel too, for it is all uncertain *where* that will be. Eva has not been feeling very well. looks harrassed & now, she frets so much about Home & you

We feel *very* anxious about Atlanta & consequently about the whole of Geo [Georgia]— Once more good bye. Kiss Hadder for Mama, & tell him I will see him soon I hope. dear precious child, I hope he keeps well. & gives as little trouble, as *possible*. Love to all, & sweet kisses from Bubba to you & Hadder. he *calls the name* very sweetly. But calls himself *Col. King* I send you the little card Photograph of B. Bubba calls it the "Pickets of a man" But you must judge *for your self*. as to the likeness— Aunt Cliff is writing so you will get the news—if there is any. Yours- Bessie

The following letter from Barrington to his father repeats the contents of previous letters that were likely slow in arriving since they were en route during the Campaign of Atlanta.

---

[250] Indispensable. Bessie intends to make diapers out of her old tablecloths.

[251] Bessie again expressed her fear of dying in childbirth.

Bismack. On Williamsburg Road

Aug 17th 1864

My Dear Father,

I have one horse for Jessy to ride, & have concluded to send him home to bring on the nurse & other things for my wife. I can spare him now better than any other time.

Please father buy a nurse for Bessie at any price. It is utterly impossible to buy or hire one here in Va. Mr. Few[252] of whom I told you the other day, has one he might hire or sell. So write to him at Thomasville, M. C. Few is his name. But please get one. any way & let her come on with Jessy. After Jessy has collected every thing do give him a pass to Staunton mentioning that he has boxes for me. Do give him money to pay expenses back, & pay him $230- that I owe him. (Two hundred and thirty dollars.) I have not time now to write much. Grant is attempting a movement on north side of James [River] again. We won in a pretty heavy skirmish yesterday. My Regt has lost a number wounded but none killed. We drove them back under cover of their gunboats. Every thing *very* quiet this morning, report says Grant is moving away rapidly. We were on our way to Culpeper the other day, but recalled to protect Richmond. Expect we will move up in a few days towards the mountains. Give much love to dear Mother & all. May our lives be spared to meet in safety earnestly prays your aftc son

B.S. King

This is the last correspondence for 1864. Perhaps the family was together for the winter. Maybe Bessie got her nurse. On 31 October 1864, Bessie gave birth to a daughter, Catherine Margaret "Maggie" King.

---

[252] M. C. Few of Thomasville GA, commissary in Cobb's Legion.

In January 1865, Barrington S. King accompanied Bessie back to Roswell and left her there with the children. He left for the front in late January. The family home, Barrington Hall, as well as the homes of the other founding families of Roswell, survived the Northern attack.

Cobb's Legion, Cavalry Battalion, was stationed in Camp Bellfield in Greenville County, Virginia, located near Bellfield around mid-January 1865.[253]

The following letter from Bessie to Barrington relates how Bessie set up housekeeping again. It is difficult to determine the identity of various people she mentions, but they were likely citizens of Roswell.

Roswell Feb 9th 1865

My own precious darling,

We will have a mail today, but I have had something like a Whitlow[254] on my right hand thumb. This has prevented my writing, ~~but~~ my hand being too sore to grasp the penholder. I will begin my first letter today, am going up to the house, & have Judy (Mr Camps woman) & Mrs. Coleman to clean up—& Well you have never, I am sure seen so much *dirt*, its perfectly *horrid*, we have nearly killed ourselves & still *you* would not *believe* any thing had been done.

---

[253] William S. Smedlund, *Camp Fires of Georgia's Troops, 1861–1865* (Lithonia GA: Kennesaw Mountain Press, 1994) 64.

[254] A flaw or sore at the quick.

Monday

Darling I am in *the house* came in on saturday & Charley[255] & Bayard[256] stay with me at night. Why dont the Maj[257] & Ralph[258] come along? Martha[259] and I do all the work, and we get along very well, by ourselves, but I will be obliged to have a cook, when the gentlemen come. Daddy Luke cuts my wood & Mr Grimes hauled me a load on saturday— very small its true, & its nearly gone. But Mr Stien promised to try & get up some today.

McCall has told *more* lies on *you* than you could shake a stick at. When they come to me with *little* I say "go away with it, *I* dont want to hear it," and wont listen to it for its too contempilible— McCall says however *that you cursed and swore* (!). & said you were going to Augusta to have one big fight, & came back here, & have 3 or 4. and thrash out *all* the Rogues etc— He does every thing he can to keep these people from helping me, but I am independent for Mrs Coleman does all my washing & scrubbling—& Old Cassels or, [illegible], either will come any time & help me. The country people are coming in constantly, & *begging* for weaving sewing of *any thing* to get yarn for work—eggs & butter in plenty, but no Lord chickens or bacon. We have a piece of Bacon that Aunt Role loaned me, & the rice you bought with some *awful flour,* & some worse hominy & plenty of eggs & some butter— We get eggs 20 doz for a bunch of your butter 10 lbs pr bunch sorguin [sorghum] 6 gals pr

---

[255] Charles Jones Pratt, son of Rev. Nathaniel Alpheus Pratt and Barrington S. King's aunt Catherine Barrington King, was born in 1842 and was the same age as Clifford Alonzo King, the youngest son of Barrington King.

[256] Eliza Barrington King, Barrington S. King's aunt, was the widow of Bayard E. Hand. This Bayard was their son.

[257] Maj. John Minton.

[258] Ralph Brown King was a brother of Barrington S. King.

[259] This was probably the same slave that was with Bessie in Virginia.

bunch. I have the offer of a barrel but declined trading, until I *saw* the article— We cook in the *pantry* (it is not much, but takes Martha a good while)—& its such a dirty place I am afraid it will never come clean. I hope you will tell me about my trunks having arrived when you write My *precious darling* can you get a Leave of absence? I very much fear *not*- so soon as you expected. I do so wish you were here, papa [Barrington S. King] to see me cooking breakfast, & little Miss[260] is lying in the Couch looking at me while I write—& cooing so sweetly she grows finely—& those blessed little arm in "satus quo—" no longer & no smaller still, I said they were with, & I am bound to *have* them little. Thurse [illegible] *logic,* a womans, any way!—

Papa when you come, you *must* bring 2 locks—one for the store soon & one for my room when I leave this— one of the women *loaned* me Mothers[261] room key— Do her good when I return it!

now I am in the house & my own arrangments & children about me & lo! I am so homesick & tired of your absence and *all* that I feel ready to halt— I *wont* as this, but truly I *feel* like it—& it would do me so much good, if you would come & let me have a good cry! I am *so* weary of having you away- & if it were not for your honor & duty in the matter, I would give out. There is nothing else, but this *nor* that *should* separate us—nothing but death! I went to our dear Bros grave,[262] & its so still & sad & sweet there, two pine trees have fallen across the enclosure, & the precious earth will now be protected from the desecration of the enemy— dont tell it but the Yankees rode all round & round it, and made their horses *paw it!* Dont mention it, for I dont

---

[260] Catherine Margaret "Maggie" is the third child of Barrington S. and Bessie and would have been a little more than three months old at the time.

[261] Mother's. She is referring to Barrington's mother, Catherine Margaret Nephew King.

[262] The grave of Thomas Edward King. He was killed at the Battle of Chickamauga on 19 September 1863.

wont Eva or Mother or dear sister Marie to hear it- They also burst open G. Fathers vault[263]—& examined *all* inside! & these are the people *Georgians* want to go back to! The news here is, that Augusta has fallen. *I* dont believe it—but we are so cut off that we have no means of knowing *anything*. I shall be so rejoiced when you come.

Wednesday— George[264] came on Monday—& stays with me— We have a very pleasent time, he praises my cooking, & we all only wish *you*. Major Minlow & Bro Jim[265] came yesterday, & they have gone to work— I hunting up things brought me my [illegible]ny fender(?) this morning, & the Maj promised me some bedding— We will be quite comfortable by the time you come— Papa I am in *real* need of a pair of shoes— if you could buy me some, I can go about the house with these I have, but they dont do for bad weather— my fine calf skin shoes are rubbed through & I am in a fix! I want too darling a *little sugar* and some coffee— no body *shall touch it*, but myself and yourself. I *would* like some 2 water pitchers & a few nails— & think I can manage———

I do long for you to come— The Maj & Bro Jim are both anxious to see you. George returns to Millegeville on Monday— The Cadets[266] have seen some real hard work- George is 3 or 4 inches taller, than I am but looks pretty rough— Bro Jim is taken

---

[263] Burial vault of Roswell King, Barrington S. King's grandfather.

[264] George was probably George MacLeod, a nephew of Bessie's. There is a George McLeod listed as a private in Company A of the Georgia Military Institute roster, also referred to as Capers Battalion Georgia Militia (*Capers Battalion Georgia Militia* <www.researchonline.net/gacw/unit140.htm> [14 May 2003]).

[265] James Roswell King was a brother of Barrington S. King.

[266] These cadets were students of the Georgia Military Institute in Marietta. They were called up to fight during the Atlanta Campaign. They were also called to protect the Capitol in Milledgeville and to help with the defenses in Savannah.

with Maggie[267]— I have got old Mom Rose[268] to help me & think we will get along pretty well. Sister Fran[269] had Hudy, Fanny & Yobell[270] sent to Macon—& it will be some time before they can be brought back.

I feel strongly tempted to have a white nurse if one can be found—so that I may have some one to rely upon should the Yankees return— I will not fear I am resolved—unless they burn me out—which I hardly anticipate. Bro Jim says Marie has gone to Europe he heard through a letter from her to sister Fran[271] of Nov. 16th of her safe arrival in "best Philadelphia"— Miss Hamilton[272] was exceedingly ill, not expected to live. Mom Rose[273] says it cause "all along of fretting about de blue Buckra"— She told me today when she saw some of my contrivances, "eh! eh!—old head an young shoulders"— She & Martha[274] get on finely & Martha just suits for this sort of

---

[267] Maggie is Catherine Margaret, the third child of Barrington S. and Bessie.

[268] Mom Rose was an elderly slave who had lived in Darien with Sarah Amanda King Walker, daughter of Reuben King who was the brother of Roswell King, on Mallow Plantation. In a letter from Sarah Walker dated November 1862 to her three sons serving in the Confederate States Army, she mentions that all the slaves were taken by the Yankees except for old Mom Rose, who was "left at the negroes houses to die alone" (Sarah Joyce King Cooper, *King and Allied Families* [Athens GA: Agee Publishers, Inc., 1992] 33).

[269] Elizabeth Frances "Fanny" Prince was the wife of James Roswell King and the sister-in-law of Bessie and Barrington S. King.

[270] The slaves were sent to Macon in hopes of keeping them away from the Northern Forces.

[271] Elizabeth Frances "Fanny" Prince.

[272] Miss Hamilton was the schoolteacher who taught young Harris earlier in the war.

[273] Mom Rose was an elderly slave having lived in Darien with Sarah Amanda King Walker, daughter of Reuben King who was the brother of Roswell King.

[274] Martha is the slave who accompanied Bessie in Virginia.

housekeeping. We will be obliged to have some *plates* for I have 8 borrowed ones now—

I wish I could get some papers, & know what you are all doing in S. Carolina.

Bayard[275] has just called for my letter & I must close— May God bless you my beloved one— I had sweet dreams of you last night— we are *all well* your own Loving Bessie

On 10 February 1865, Inspector General John G. Devereux reported on the cavalry commands in Georgia and South Carolina. He recounted the events of the previous summer when Roswell fell, focusing on the cavalry movements. Captain James R. King was ordered to report to Brig. General M. J. Wright after the fall of Roswell. Wright made the battalion a permanent company and ordered that they turn their artillery over to the arsenal in Atlanta, and he made them a mounted company. Although they were mustered as mounted, many of the men never received horses. After the fall of Atlanta, Captain King was ordered to report to General Howell Cobb, who assigned the company to General Alfred Iverson, who in turn assigned them to Hannon's brigade. The arms used by the company were varied widely and in short supply.[276]

The following is part of a letter, page 5, written by Bessie to Barrington. The envelope was dated 20 February and postmarked in Macon, Georgia. The address on the envelope reads "Lt. Col. B.S. King, Cavalry Cobbs Legion, Youngs Brigade, Columbus, S. Carolina." This letter was written in 1865.

---

[275] Eliza Barrington King, aunt of Barrington S. King, was the widow of Bayard Hand. This Bayard was their son.

[276] *OR,* ser. 1, vol. 47, pt. 2, p. 1152.

Page 5th

Ralph[277] & I get on very pleasently and quietly, agreeing as we do, on the questions of the day—you *know* how I feel—coming to Geo—[Georgia] has not yet *demoralized* me—as they all threatened— No! & if I know myself, nothing *can* do that—I do not know *what* I should do if the Yankees were to come here- I am [illegible] struck at the very thought—but I would try very hard to be a brave *good* soldiers wife—and not disgrace my name and country—Why dont some of you come home & hang Gov. Brown,[278] he certainly seem trying to *test* the forbearance of the Constitution and demonstrate to his *own* satisfaction, the definition of "Treason"—he can never give up Georgia—our loved ones lie buried here—our children were born here—& *here* we _____[279] we shall die, when all troubles cease—& the *weary rest*— This being the feeling of so many good people, *we must* & will keep Georgia—in spite of Joseph E. Brown—who is a villain and ought to be hung. I have so many many things to tell you & ask you & my heart is so *homesick* when I stop to think that I wont know what to do—. I generally work very hard & never give myself time to worry—& I can do *that*, (work) without hunting for it.

Charley[280] is come—& will leave in a few moments. May God in heaven bless you my beloved one. & strenghten & nerve

---

[277] Ralph Brown King, Barrington S. King's brother.

[278] Joseph E. Brown was first elected governor of Georgia in 1857 and was reelected in 1859, 1861, and 1863. Brown disagreed with the way President Davis ran the government and the way he conducted war (Boatner, *Civil War Dictionary,* 91–92).

[279] Corner of letter missing.

[280] Charles Jones Pratt, son of Rev. Nathaniel Alpheus Pratt and Barrington S. King's aunt Catherine Barrington King, was born in 1842 and

you for *all* that may be before you. I send you a sweet little violet. I have made a bed just by the steps & close to the Piazza[281]—& *you* shall have the *first* bloom. They are so sweet. We are all well & Mother & children unite in prayers for the darling we all miss so sadly—.

Your own Loving Bessie—

❖

The following is a letter to Barrington S. King from Bessie King. This letter demonstrates her love for him and offers details on how she ran the household.

❖

Roswell Feb 24th 1865.

My own darling,

I will write now & get Charley Pratt,[282] who leaves us in a day or two to carry my letter. & mail from Athens— Oh! my own beloved one, you dont know how terrible it is, to think we may not be able to hear from each other. I dont think I can *stand* it! The long weary days will be more than *I* can bear! I received your letter of the 4th from Athens. & am so sorry you had such a dreadful time. It was very hard on you my *poor darling soldier boy*! Oh! papa if it could only end, & our independence be *established!* & you come home— Oh! *joy* for us, now & hereafter. I dream sweet dreams, of you *every night,* & it cheers me up—instead of making me unhappy—. We have no mails here—& they send once in 10 days- I thought they were to

---

was the same age as Clifford Alonzo King, the youngest son of Barrington King.

[281] Large, covered porch.

[282] Barrington's cousin.

send on Saturday, but they sent today—& I see Wheeler[283] has been whipping old *Rills*. I have so much to tell you. I am now fixed pretty well—only sleeping very *un*comfortably on one *old* hard mattress—would put it on the floor but am afraid it would give Baby a cold— She is so very beautiful & bright—coos and laughs. & has a good old time of it. You will love her more than ever, when you come. She grows finely too, and seems to be teething, bless her pretty heart. grows more like mother[284] every day—

I have a fine cow now—gives 2 gallons pr day. We gave 800—in money—which I think was doing well— Calf 6 weeks old—male— she is very gentle—& well disposed. I get Mrs Coleman to milk for me. She helps me very much indeed. We think of hiring a woman in Atlanta— her husband belongs to the factory & Ralph, who come up on Saturday last brought him up. I could have Fanny,[285] out from *all* accounts, she is impertinence, & I dont want her. They are all down at Macon, & would not be satisfied probably. so let them be hired out— Bill[286] is here & is a nuisance. & makes more trouble for me, than he helps— I told Ralph to put *him*. to work for the Factory, & let me have Sandy for gardener. R. says—*he* cant hire men—to work for you- & means to put in a crop for himself- he has no settled place, that I can see, & from my heart, I wish *you were here*, you must get a

---

[283] Gen. Joseph "Fighting Joe" Wheeler, CSA, was commissioned first lieutenant and was then named colonel of 19th Alabama. He was appointed brigadier general on 30 October 1862 and was made major general on 20 January 1863. July 1863 he was given command of the cavalry of the entire Army of Mississippi in order to perform raids on Federal communications. He fought in the Knoxville siege, the Atlanta Campaign, the March to the Sea, and through the Carolinas (Boatner, *Civil War Dictionary,* 910).

[284] Like Barrington's mother, Catherine Margaret Nephew King.

[285] Fanny was a slave of the King family. She was among the remaining slaves sent to Macon GA to keep them from the Union Army.

[286] Bill was another slave of the King family.

furlough & come up *my darling*—and start matters right— I can
do nothing— the fact is Ralph wants to plant the garden, & send
it— he wants to make a regular crop—& I dont think he will do
anything— "Too many *irons* in *the* fire"— He is detailed to
work for the factory interests—& cant in my estimation do
both. I do want *you* to come—& let me have a boy or girl about
the house to do my little errands— Mom Rose[287] is going
soon—& I will have no one, till we get the woman from Atlanta.
& Martha will nurse. but I must have some one to do little things
for me—& you were very fortunate in not buying Maj. Minton's
negroes— Aunt Kate[288] says its Binah he wished to sell you—& a
more torn down piece never lived—. No one can live with her—
If I had a good white girl to nurse—& help me sew, & so one—I
could manage *well* with Martha—but if you get one, *remember*
you must not make *any more bargains*, but just let her
understand, that I shall have need or help in *various* ways—&
not come as Cynthia did— "*I* did not *engage* to do this, & Peasy
said I was not to do that"[289]— But she must do any & every
thing *that* comes to hand— *I* wont *over work any body*— I cook
first rate though its not my choice of an occupation, I can do
it—& George[290] who staid week with me was quite delighted with
it— Jim Dalton told the Servants & G. Mothers,[291] that he must
get away from Ma [Bessie]— before Col. B. King came—for he
was afraid of your killing him! Oh! I *do* wish you were here. You
have no fear of these cowardly Crackers—& they *are* terror

---

[287] Elderly slave.

[288] Aunt Kate was Catherine Barrington King, wife of Reverend Nathaniel
Alpheus Pratt and aunt of Barrington S. King.

[289] Apparently Barrington S. King had made promises to slaves regarding
the type of work they would be required to do. Bessie suffered from these
promises as she tried to run the house with slaves who were exempt from
particular activities.

[290] George MacLeod, a nephew of Bessie's.

[291] Her mother and her husband's mother.

struck at you very *name*— I have much to tell you. & only wish you were here, *now* to recover things, which *soon* will be beyond your reach— I see by the papers that our dear old Genl Hampton has been placed in command at Co—& I trust that he will organize & arrange matters a little. They must be sadly in want of it. George did not know what to do—go into Infantry or Scouts—but *prefers* Cavalry—only he has no horse. I tell him I think its as *little* as G. M. can do to buy him one. Dont you?

The little boys want you home and talk about it a great deal—& say they must show you the pretty new cow & calf & little sister— They have as much milk as they care to drink twice a day—poor little fellow—they want your training sadly— I feel my own utter want of it— Things would have been very different if you had never left me to my own unguided will— God knows it grieves me sorely enough when my ways are a cause of unhappiness to you—*but oh!* the *will* the spirit within me! is too much for me. It would *all be well* if you could be at home- with this care of the *bitter* struggle off your mind—& you could be *with me,* as you were before, to [illegible], but not condemn me for my faults— I should *never* be too old to leave goodness & gentleness from your example— I have strong faith & hope that you will be spared for my good. that even if the prime of our days should be spent in this separation, our *last* days may like Jobs[292] be our best— God *knows* we both need help. only your nature & mine are so totally *different*— I need something strong & *tender* like *you* to sustain my feeble good intentions—you perhaps, need a *little* of my vivacity—& *all* my sympathy and I know I want *all your* love & kind forbearance—for I am *very very feeble*—as a Christian—& my darling if our hearts are right for the hereafter, *all* will be well, no matter *what* we pass through in this world— It may be, hard & bitter trials are yet before us—

---

[292] Job's. The biblical character Job suffered many trials to test his faith.

But my faith in the final issue is as *bright* as unclouded, as unswerving as on the day you went into our noble Army.

> *Night* may *seem* to be *right,* but
> it is only for a day—

I will have everything nice by the time you come. & you are to enjoy your self *good* when you come. & see *all* are going to be *very happy.* my own darling

The following letter is from Barrington to Bessie.

Camp near Charlotte N.C.

Feb 24th 1865

My own precious best beloved

A time so long has passed since I wrote my last letter that it seems *months*. It is nearly two weeks any way, & I know your *dear* heart must be worried almost crazy to know what has become of the "old man," because although I can picture you in health & comparitive comfort in the homested, yet 3 weeks have gone by without my hearing a word from or about you, & my mind is *not* at ease regarding you & the dear little ones. But what must *you* feel who have been hearing exagerated accounts of our fighting particularly Youngs Brigade.[293] The fact is my darling we are retreating *without* fighting & Sherman[294] is, in fact *now* march through S.C. as easily as he did through Georgia. I will go rapidly over the incidents of the past two weeks now, merely as a reminder when the war ends, to be enlarged upon when we can converse. I rejoined the command on Monday as I told you I would. & the next day threw up breastworks for the protection of

[293] Pierce Manning Butler Young's (P. M. B.) brigade.

[294] William T. Sherman, US General.

Columbia [South Carolina]. Kept in the ditches that night raining & freezing as it fell. All next day Wednesday was occupied in strengthening our works, we were on the right. Some skirmishing all day on the left. Sherman to save his ammunition would not press on but moved up across the Saluda [South Carolina] river, thereby causing us to fall back across the Congarce [Congaree River, South Carolina] which was done Wednesday night & the long bridge burned. Thursday the Yankees kept moving up the river all day in plain view from Columbia. Slight skirmishing was kept up all day across the river. The Yankees very sparing of ammunition, but they could not resist the temptation of firing a few shell at the new capitol[295] 3 of which struck the end towards the river defacing it very little. Thursday night was occupied by our Brigade in being remounted & armed. I did not sleep one wink that night. All knew the place was to be evacuated the next morning & the stores were rapidly being plundered by soldiers & citizens. I will tell you all about this when we meet. At day light we moved down of the left & at 8 A M recd orders to move up rapidly to Columbia our Regt was in front of the Divn [Division] moving at a gallop through the street running parrellel with Main St, when we got to the street that Mrs Bronsons home is on the yankees were coming in on Main St. We took the right there, passing by the Insane asylum. Words can not describe my feelings at seeing Ladies and children running about wild with excitement & fear, ringing there hands & crying. & the few that could control themselves, telling us to fight to the end although compelled to retreat now never give up & other words of cheer. There was not a man but gripped his sabre the tighter & felt more than ever determined *never* to give up this struggle till

---

[295] South Carolina State Capitol had been a long project, having begun on 15 December 1851 when the state laid the cornerstone. Work had progressed over the next decade and a half when Sherman's army fired upon the building on 17 February 1865, damaging it only slightly (*SC State House History* <www.scstatehouse.net-LPITR> [5 July 2001])).

liberty or *death* be our lot. Our Regt was divided here by Genl Hampton.[296] Col Wright[297] taking half & going in front with Genl Butler,[298] & I was left in the street with drawn sabres ready to charge should the Yankees make any demonstration, with orders to remain till every thing had passed out. I was the last of any organized force to leave the city, a few stragglers came dashing along, the Yanks firing at them from behind. When we go out to the College (Barhanville)[299] I was ordered to remain there until I had sent 4 men back to the Charlotte [North Carolina] depôt to burn it. 4 good men more picked out & in a half hour I saw the black smoke rising up. A large amount of ammunition was in the depôt. It is terrible what heavy losses individuals & the government met with in giving up that place. It seemed to me that nothing was attempted to save anything until too late. Friday night the Yankees destroyed by fire 3/4 of the city. I can not find out what parts were destroyed but expect your trunk & yarn was all destroyed. Prisoners say it was accidental but we can believe as much of that as we please. We kept on retreating every day the Yankees keeping up as we gave back. Until Wednesday this disease which I have all along thought to be camp itch,[300] became unendurable & the surgeon sent me off to Charlotte where I reached last night & am now using iodine ointment & taking arsenic (Fowlers solution) ointment. I am better already. It is *not* itch I am happy to state but a much more itching eruption a species of Herpes. I will soon be well. The Regt [regiment] & Divn are gradually falling back & will be here tomorrow. This place will also be evacuated every body in

---

[296] Gen. Wade Hampton.

[297] Col. Gilbert J. Wright.

[298] Matthew Calbraith Butler, CSA.

[299] Barhamville College in Columbia SC was a women's college in existence from 1817–1861.

[300] Condition caused by insects or skin disease (www.ehistory.com/uscw/features/medicine/cwsurgeon/introduction.cfm).

leaving & taking every thing. Oh what terrible suffering there must have been in Columbia that *horrible* night. A stand will be made before long, & Sherman will as certainly be whipped if he does not fall back to Charleston. Every thing is being prepared to fire him & he will God willing meet his deserts. I dont know when I will be able to get my leave of absence my *precious darling* my heart *yearns* to be with you, to *know* that you are comfortable & to help you fix up. It is hard to know that we are cut off from all communication with each other & weeks may yet pass before mail communication is resumed, but we must *endure* this as we have *other* trials & pray God it may not be long before we meet in safety & health again. Kiss my *precious* little ones God *bless them* & *you* my *hearts darling* keeping you from *all* suffering harm or bitter trials. I am *very* anxious to hear about Father & Mother. Give love to Uncle, Aunt & cousins. I will send this the first opportunity *your own*.

Barrington

The following letter is from Barrington to Bessie.

At Mr Morris [unknown] near Charlotte   Feb 28th 1865
My own *precious darling* wife,
After writing to you on Sunday the weather got so bad I sent Jessy[301] off to find a house near by that I could stay at & the name at the top is that of the man where I am now staying. I was well that I left the wagon camp for I have escaped some miserable weather & am also by being in a house very rapidly getting over this skin disease.[302] I hope now that by the end of

---

[301] Slave of Barrington S. King.
[302] Herpes he described in his last letter.

this week I will again be fit for duty. With the exception of the skin my health is excellent & am perfectly well. I have not one particle of news to tell you. The Yankees are in Lancaster Dist [South Carolina] & making their way toward Wilmington [North Carolina]. I dont know where the command is but the wagons are yet encamped near here.

My *precious one* I have been thinking *much* of you & our little ones lately & have become *very* anxious to hear from you to *know* how you are getting along in Roswell. I sometimes fear Ralph nor Maj Minton[303] have gone there & that you are yet at Uncle Pratts[304] with no prospect of getting fixed in the old home housekeeping.

My mind is troubled to think that you *may* not be comfortable, or, *actually suffering* from want of *necessaries* of life. I wish *so much* I could hear from you. Nearly 4 weeks have gone by now since I left you in Roswell & it may be a long time yet before I can hear any thing from you. Oh! that peace *could* be ours, that in a *home* of *our own* I could devote my *time, energy* & *life* for *your happiness* & *comfort* my heart *more* capable having *greater* cause to *love* you my *best beloved my chosen wife of my bosom.* Oh that God would in mercy *answer* our prayers. I have not been able to see Harry Pratt[305] not being able to ride but sent him a message yesterday & hope he will come to see me. I dont know that I told you of having sent one bale of yarn to Mr Bedill (at Columbia) to be sold. I dont know whether it was sold, stolen or burnt. I thought it best to sell one & risk the other at Mrs Baldwins but am afraid all has been lost. I can find out in a few days all about it I hope.

---

[303] Maj. John Minton.

[304] Reverend Nathaniel Alpheus Pratt, husband of Catherine Barrington King and thus uncle of Barrington S. King.

[305] Henry Barrington Pratt was a cousin of Barrington S. King, son of Reverend Nathaniel Alpheus Pratt and Catherine Barrington King.

How my heart *yearns* in its loneliness to *hold you close to my breast my darling my precious wife*. I have *so much* to *love* you for God grant we may *yet* live together as *before* the war with *increased* & *pure sweet love* for each other & be *once* more *happy so very happy* I *know* I fail to *show* you my love & have at times made you *unhappy* with my petulance and selfishness. But God knows *I love you* with *all* the *best* & *strongest* feelings. I am capable of, & that *you* are *more worthy* of it than *any* person in the world. I will *try* & curl my own *mean* & *weak* points of character when next we meet & *show* you *all* the love which is in my heart & which *you* so *well* deserve.

Kiss my *precious* little ones dear little lambs how I *long* to see them *precious little Maggie* particularly, she is 4 months old now & must be *more* sweet than ever. God *bless* them & *you* my *hearts darling* my *precious wife* & keep us *all* in safety through *all* dangers permitting us to meet in safety in due season *earnestly prays*

Your *own much loving* husband
B.S. King

The following letter is from Barrington to Bessie.

At Mr Morris near Charlotte

March 2nd 1865

My own precious darling

Out of habit & the great desire to converse with you through the medium which has afforded me so much consolation in the long years of our separation, I write again to day, although I feel almost certain my letters will never reach you. My anxiety to hear from you is getting more & more great & my mind more & more troubled. I try to make myself *believe* that you are all well & happy in the old home. But fears & doubts will arise & make me feel unhappy, & my being inactive & confined to the house, has a tendency to make me feel gloomy low spirited & very homesick. This eruption [herpes] is almost well now, if it will only remain so. I will leave for the command ready for duty by monday next anyway. I hope it will not come out again but am afraid the cure is only temporary. If it comes out any more after I return to duty I shall go before the medical board for a furlough. The people of the home are very kind & do every thing to make me comfortable. There are no young ladies here only a young girl about 14 years. Perhaps if there were some here I could be cheered up & made to feel less gloomy. But what I want *most* is to be with *you my precious one best beloved* with our children, bless them. & until I *hear* from you I can not feel any thing but gloomy. There is no news. The Yankees are unable to move on account of the mud it having rained more or less for 6 days & is still drizzling, dark clouds hanging low with prospects of more rain. The roads are in a terrible condition, red clay like Cobb Co [Georgia], & cut up deep with mine. No one seems to know where Sherman will move to whether Wilmington or Lynchburg or Charleston. He is making a demonstration against this place now at Monroe Union Co [North Carolina]. His main army is in Lancaster Dist.

My *precious darling* I feel *this* separation from you more than at any time before. Leaving you to go to housekeeping with *nothing* & if I could *only* be with you we could be *more* happy than ever before. God grant you are well & comfortable & *keep* you so till we meet which I pray may not be *far* in the future. Give love to all. Kiss my *precious* little children, with a heart *full* of *pure strong love* for *you dearest* & *best* of all *earthly* love I am

Your *much loving* husband
B.S. King

The following letter is from Barrington to Bessie.

Camp near Charlotte March 3rd1865

My own precious darling

I have recovered sufficiently from this eruption [herpes] as to be fit for duty again, & will in a short time leave for the command hoping to be near them by night.

I am rejoiced to hear there is a regular mail communication opened yesterday between this place & Georgia, either Athens [Georgia] or Washington, [DC]. We will be able therefore after a few days to hear with some regularity from each other much to our mutual gratification I know. The command has been in a fight lately two of my old company were killed Shaw[306] living near Roswell was one the other Mahaffy of Gwinnett. If possible let Mrs. Shaw know They were killed in a charge on Shermans waggons three days ago. I cant hear the particulars. You will see in the papers a correspondence between Sherman & Genl Hampton about killing Shermans foragers. None are taken prisoners but all killed. I am afraid my *darling wife* that I will not be able to get any furlough this spring, as long as the campaign continues active I will not apply, as I will be needed with the command.

May God in mercy grant us a *happy union with each other before many weeks*. Give love to all. I would give so *much* to be at home for a short time *dearest* to assist you. But you will have to do without my presence & help. I have the 2 mares for you, but am afraid to send them through the country now with Jessy. Do the best you can & may God enable us to say from our *hearts* "His will be done" & may his grace sustain us to bear *unmurmuringly* the dispensations of his providence. Kiss my *precious* little darlings with a *good* hug for Madge [Maggie]. May the blessings of God *rest* on *them* & on *you best beloved* sparing

---

[306] J. Sidney Shaw served in Cobb's Legion, Company E.

all our lives & health to live *long* & *happily* together when this
war shall end, ever prays your *own much loving* husband

B.S. King

THE SOUTHERN TELEGRAPH COMPANIES
[printed notifications and terms omitted]
[no date]
By telegraph from Raleigh 23 via Ca To Capt J.R. King[307]

Dispatch received Lt. Col. B. S. King was killed in a charge
at Johnsonville N.C. on 11th inst[308] will write particulars

Thos H. Williams
Maj. & [illegible]

❖

The following letter is from James Roswell King to Bessie
regarding to newspaper list of Barrington being wounded and of
him being killed.

❖

Macon 21 Mch 1865

My dear Bessy
I wrote you immediately on Seeing the two notices in the
papers of our Brother [Barrington], I know you would be in a
State of great agony of mind. We have no farther news at all &
keep indulging in a hope that he may be only wounded. I have

---

[307] Captain James Roswell King was a brother of Barrington S. King.

[308] Abbreviation for instant, which means of the current month
(*Webster's New Twentieth Century Dictionary of the English Language*,
unabridged, 2d ed. [New York: The World Publishing Company, 1971]).

telegraphed to all the Sources, I think I can get any farther information from, and am still without any news. Bill [slave] came last night. I kept him to day to see if any thing would come. I send him back & will send you the very first information we get. If I can get suitable papers I will go on myself and look after him. It would be next to impossible for you to get on these now. I will do all in my power for him & if wounded will contrive him some way of getting to Geo. [Georgia] or make him comfortable where he is. I feel greatly for you my dear sister & trust you will find support in this dark hour of suspense. I have not written Father & Mother yet until we can find out the facts.

Your aff Bro.
J.R. King

The following correspondence was written on the back of the proceeding one. It was written by James Roswell King's wife, Fanny Prince King.

My dear Bessie

I cannot let Bill [slave] go back without writing you a line to assure you of my great sympathy for you in this trying time of suspense— I have felt very deeply for you since we saw the name in the paper among the wounded, I know your feelings for I went thro' it all last ~~summer~~ winter when my own dear Husband was hurt, a man then *told* Dr Green [unknown] he had *seen* James fall from his horse after being shot, & he came home at last safe, God grant our dear Brother [Barrington S. King] may also come thro' this safely, James has spared no pains to find out *every* thing & I do hope you may be rewarded for this trying time of suspense by the glad tidings of his welfare, a lady in Macon whose husband was in Va heard of his death, & mourned him for 2 weeks, when he came home *safe* having been left for dead or otherwise overlooked— do, dear Bessie brave up, if you think you would like to be here, I shall be most happy to have you at our house—we have a room at your disposal. Kiss you dear little ones for me. Give my love to Aunt Kate Pratt[309]—& Uncle[310] & the girls & ever believe me in trust sympathy

Your aff sister F.P. King

Barrington King had moved to Savannah during the war and was still there when news of Barrington Simeral King's death came to the family. In a letter dated 23 March 1865 published in a secondary source, Barrington King wrote to his daughter-in-law, Florence, wife of Ralph Brown King, about their fears of the unconfirmed death. Florence, Florrie, or Flora as she is referred to in this letter, had traveled to New York and arrived safely on the second day of the month. Barrington has seen the misprinted name, "B.L. King," in the paper and felt that it was his son. However, they were holding out hope since they were not permitted to receive letters from outside the lines and although some had been brought from Macon they were delivered and destroyed by orders. According to his letter, Bessie was keeping house for Ralph and Major John Minton.[311]

The following letter is from James R. King to Reverend Nathaniel Alpheus Pratt.

---

[309] Catherine Barrington King was the sister of Barrington King and wife of Reverend Nathaniel Alpheus Pratt, thus aunt of Barrington S. King's aunt.

[310] Reverend Nathaniel Alpheus Pratt.

[311] Coleman, *A Short History,* 50.

Macon 27 March 1865

My dear Uncle,

I deeply regret to announce the death of Another beloved Brother in this cruel war. I enclose you the telegram. I recd in reply to one sent Maj Genl Young[312] care of Lieut Genl Hampton,[313] Raliegh, N.C. It has been some time in reaching me in Consequence of the wares [telegraph wires] being down. I wrote Bessy immediately on Seeing the two reports both official, one reporting that he was Killed. & the other wounded hoping that the latter would prove the correct news in the end, but alas, it is not so. & the Sad and Severe stroke has fallen upon us again. I write you to ~~got~~ get you to See poor Bessy and break the Sad, Sad, news to her. I have felt for her much in her anxiety and suspense, but more, far more, in her sad bereavement. May our Heavenly Father support her in this dark hour.

I will probably get the particulars soon & send them on to her. I will write Maj Williams [Thomas H. Williams] to have his effects sent me & his boy[314]—as soon as possible. I will write him my self. much love to her & you all. all well.

Your aff neph.
J.R. King

---

[312] Pierce Manning Butler Young.

[313] Gen. Wade Hampton.

[314] The "boy" is Jessy, the slave who accompanied Barrington S. King through the war.

The following is the official account of what happened to Barrington Simeral King.

❖

Hd Qs Youngs Co Brig-[315]
March 29th 1865

Mrs Col King[316]

Madam

As Jessie[317] is going home I thought My duty as the friend & brother officer of your deceased husband to write you, giving the particulars of his death.

Col King Returned to the command from the Hospital at Charlotte N.C. (where he had been for a few days with slight illness) on the 9th inst.[318] on the morning of the 10th our brigade was ordered to charge the camp of the Yankee Genl Kilpatrick,[319] The Cobb Legion under Col King led the charge which was entirely Successful until the enemy rallied & the Cobb Legion again charged the Yankee Battery in which charge the

---

[315] Headquarters, Young's Company Brigade.

[316] Mrs. Colonel King (Bessie).

[317] Slave of Barrington S. King.

[318] Abbreviation for instant, which means of the current month.

[319] Gen. William Mather Kilpatrick, U.S., was commissioned as captain of 5th New York and was promoted to lieutenant colonel of the 2nd New York Cavalry on 25 September 1861. He participated in raids and skirmishes at Carmel Church, Brandy Station, Freeman's Ford, Sulphur Springs, Waterloo Bridge, Thoroughfare Gap, and Haymarket and in the second battle of Bull Run. He was named colonel of 2nd New York Cavalry on 6 December 1862 and made brigadier general on 13 June 1863. Commanding the 3rd division Cavalry Corps, Potomac, he fought at Hanover, Hunterstown, and Gettysburg. During the Atlanta Campaign, he fought at Ringgold and Dalton, where he was wounded. He commanded the 3rd Division, which was Sherman's cavalry force during the March to the Sea and the Carolinas campaign (Boatner, *Civil War Dictionary,* 459–60).

Col Recd a mortal wounded while *most* gallantly leading his men in the fight. when I first met him he was speachless therefore, I did not hear his last words. I learned from those who were very near him at the time that his last Remark was, *(Say to My wife I die willingly defending My country).*

I trust Madam that you will accept My Sincere Sympathy in your great very great bereavement, You have lost a *Kind good* husband, I a *true & tried* friend, and our common country a *staunch & noble* patriot. I would that the blow could have fallen on one whose Services to their country were less valuable, but such is the fate of war, her victims are the noblest spirits.

I trust Madam that you May have the fortitude to bear your loss as becomes the wife of So brave & noble a man,

Again I tender you My heart felt Sympathies, & believe Me Madam I remain

Your true friend
G J Wright Col
Comdg [commanding]

PS

I Send by Jessie all the Effects of Col King that I can find. I have had but little time to look to them as we have been Marching & fighting nearly every day since his death. I send his effects to his brother Capt C A King[320] on Genl Hardees[321] Staff. G. J. W.

---

[320] Clifford Alonzo King was the youngest son of Barrington King, thus Barrington S. King's younger brother.

[321] Gen. William Joseph Hardee, CSA, was appointed brigadier general on 17 June 1861 and promoted to major general on 7 October 1861. His corps participated in Shiloh, Perryville, Stones River, Missionary Ridge, and the Atlanta Campaign. Hardee gained the title of lieutenant general on 10 October 1862. In September 1864 he was given the command of the Department of South Carolina, Georgia, and Florida. He was unable to match the strength of

On a small scrap of paper the following was written and enclosed with the previous correspondence.

Effects of Lt Col B S King of the Cobb Legion Cav Small Horse & Equipments Gold Watch & Chain purse, containing $59 1/2 in Confederate treasury notes, 30cts in silver, Confederate Bond of $400.00, Haversack & Contents

Macon 30 March 1865

My Dear Sister

I know not how to Express my feelings in this Second great loss that has fallen upon our family a beloved Brother, affectionate Son and above all a devoted Husband & Father has been taken from us. I did hope when I wrote you immediately on Seeing the two notices[322] of Lieut Coln "B.L. King" Knowing that it refered to him notwithstanding the Light Error in the name but trusted all along that he was only wounded. But alas! it was a hope in vain. For the dispatch I Enclosed Uncle Pratt[323] to Communicate to you, but the sad intelligence that he "fell in a charge on the Enemy on the 11th inst.[324] at Johnsonville N.C." [illegible] that they would write the particulars. which has not yet been recd I am looking for it daily tho' it may be Sent direct to you. Can it be that we shall never more hear his deliberate voice, nor See his manly form again on Earth? Who Can tell the

---

Gen. William T. Sherman's forces and evacuated Savannah on 18 December 1864. He left Charleston in January 1865 (Boatner, *Civil War Dictionary,* 374).

[322] In the newspapers.

[323] Reverent Nathaniel Alpheus Pratt.

[324] Abbreviation for instant, which means of the current month.

amount of bitter anguish that has been wrung from devoted hearts during the Existence of this cruel war! I am forced to Exclaim My God! when, when, Shall these things Cease, & *where* shall we be, when they are accomplished?

I know you feel great anxiety to get all the particulars. and if it were possible to go on yourself to obtain them, but it is almost an impossibility to travel at all in that section of the County. I hope soon to hear all & let you have it. I desire to do all I can to make you comfortable, and if you lack for any thing let me Know & will try and supply it. or if you would like to make a change for some weeks before the warm weather Sets in, we would be very glad to have you come down & pay us a visit.

Our ground of hope that I have that his remains were properly cared for. was that the fight was a great Success to us. and he did not fall into the hands of the Enemy. and being but few casualties on our side. they could devote more time & attention to to our Killed & wounded— I trust you will find support by reposing yourself in the hands of our Saviour who has promised to be all things to us.— It only teaches us to live more loosely by the world— we are not like those who mourn without hope for we have reason to believe & hope that his has been a happy Exchange of worlds & that the two Brothers who fill the patriot's grave are together in the full fruition of Heaven, where we all trust to join them soon. May God of his gracious goodness & Mercy Support you in this dark hour & deep affliction My dear Sister in the prayer of your Bro

J. R. King[325]

as soon as I get the particulars will write some notice for the papers

---

[325] James R. King, brother of Barrington S. King.

Curtright, April 7, 1865

My dear friend

It is a heart trial at all times to approach the subjects of houshold bereavments, and that sentiments is agravated when the occasion embraces a cherished, valued, object—such is the case now—and it appears almost intrusive to offer sympathy at a time your heart and mind are so necessarily engaged contemplating your great loss— *Your* loss is not only a severe, terrible, one—but your country has lost a brave and gallant defender—one who could be poorly spared in this time of national anxiety and perils—and it appears to us inexplicable, that Providence should take from us those who are so truly valuable, yet He *does* do what is right. He *does* chastise for our good- He cannot do wrong, and He *will* open the full fountains of consolation to you in your day of distress. His Ear is never heavy, His hand ever full, fills to overflowing, with rich blessings, and though He smites, we can Kiss the nods knowing every thing worketh good to those who love Him.

Only last week I recvd from Clifford[326] the letter I now enclose to you, you have perhaps not heard the particulars he furnishes, and as they will contribute to your consolation I send it with the prayer that your mind may be led to entire submission to this grievous affliction—and that you may uncomplainingly bow your stricken souls to the righteous will of your Heavenly Father— Your trials have just begun, and they can be mitigated by such submission, and what a great blessing is yet left you in the interesting little immortalities entrusted to your guidance and direction,[327] how fearfully interesting the charge and how full of gratitude should you be that there precious gifts are left, to

---

[326] Clifford Alonzo King was the youngest son of Barrington King, thus Barrington S. King's younger brother.

[327] Author refers to the three children of Barrington and Bessie.

cluster around, and warm, your wounded chilled affections— Look aloft—cheerfully—hopefully—bravely, and with an eye of faith, and heart of submissive love, rest your future upon Him who is the firm foundation, the christian anchor.

Barrington was my friend and brother,—Evas[328] brother—and I watched his course with interest—that course has ended in glory, and the trial is now with the survivors. We must yield acquiescense to the Providence— I feel for the afflicted Parents—for our sweet sister Eva—for all survivors, may all be purified by the trial and made better prepared for that inheritance which is now high—

Submitting you to the guidance of our one comforter

I am sincerely,
Your friend
Geo H Camp[329]

Columbia S.C. April 19th/65

Mrs B.S. King

Dear Madam Yours of the 6th is just at hand and I hasten to reply I deeply regret to hear of the affliction which your letter would imply, and trust that I have misunderstood your letter, and that your kind Husband is at least Safe in person. I have seen no account of danger to him; if however my conjectures are try may God in his infinite mercy, guide, direct & protect you in this your greatest misfortune. Believe me my Dear Madam that I deeply sympathize with you in your afflictions, and the greatest of all earthly consolations to which I can point you, is that afforded by the religion which you profess. Words of consolation from friends are but thrusts which reopen the wounds and I therefore

---

[328] Catherine Evelyn "Eva" King Baker, sister of Barrington S. King.

[329] George H. Camp served in the cavalry with the Roswell Battalion.

refrain from using them but leave you in the hands of your Heavenly Father who in His own good time will assuage the grief which He has seen fit to afflict you. Your assumptions in reference to the safety of your Trunk are correct, through the Providence of God the roof which Shelters me was saved, and I am happy to say that your trunk is now in my possession, and I would willingly send it to you, if I had the opportunity, but there is not communication with Augusta except by Wagons and I Know of no going at present. You ask me if I think it safe to send it. I answer that I do not think it Safe to Send any thing any where, as the enemy are within striking where distance of us from several points, nor do we Know what day they may make a raid upon us. I do not feel at liberty to take the responsibility of shipping this Trunk to you; and shall there fore await your answer ordering sent and in the mean time I will Keep a look out for some conveyance by which it may be got to Augusta. Much has transpired in your Section of the Country since yours was written, and it may be that you may not yourself think it Safe; however when you write again, let me Know your wishes in the matter, and I shall use my best exertions to obey them. I will not weary you with a recital of our Sufferings here, you have enough of your own, besides you have seen enough of the general sufferings of our people in the Papers, without my going into details Trusting that my reply will meet with your approbation, and with the assurance on my part that I will use my feeble efforts for your welfare and with words of sympathy for your grief and prayers for the health peace & prosperity of your Family I remain Yours in the "Mistic" bond

W.T. Walters[330]

---

[330] Possibly W. T. Walters of the Georgia 10th Infantry Regiment, which served with the Army of Northern Virginia.

Please excuse this scrawl. I am quite unwell having just
finished a journey of 75 miles on foot.

The Civil War ended April 9, 1865 with General Robert E.
Lee signing the surrender at Appomattox Courthouse.

                                             Macon May 1st 1865
Col B. S. King,
In acct with Mitchel & Smiths
    ~ Cr ~
By his share of proceeds of Cards   900.80
" " " " " " Wire   2,243.75
                                              3,144.55
E. E.

Recd C.S.[331] Money from M&Smiths upd[332] sum $1700 &
placed in that $1700 of 7.30

The last part was written in different handwriting and in
pencil. This receipt indicates the money that was being spent to
get the mills producing again.

The following letter was from Marie, the other widowed
sister-in-law, to Bessie.

---

[331] Confederate States.

[332] Mitchel & Smiths unpaid.

Phila Sept 24th 1865.

My dearest Bessie,

Your letter which you sent to me ~~from~~ at Huntsville [Alabama] was forwarded & reached me a few days ago. You say that if "the powers that be" knew of the fact that your letter was written by one who never had taken the oath[333] & never intended to I might never receive it. Perhaps not,—as your humble servant stands in the same predicament. I can assure you I rejoiced in spirit when I left Huntsville behind me, with the happy consciencness that I had never had the oath offered to me, & had never been arrested & dragged before the Freedmen's Bureau on *negro testimony*[334]—both of which things often occurred to the ladies of H— [Huntsville]. I kept my quiet I can assure you.

I did not speak to a soldier the whole time I was in H— & never had one to speak to me.

Am I not a fortunate woman? I am very glad to hear that Mama is so much improved.

I had a letter from Sue Thirston [unknown] yesterday, saying that Cousin Robert[335] had been removed to Fort Lafayette—N.Y. Harbor[336]—& she & Cousin Anna[337] had been to N.Y. to make an attempt to see him, in which they had failed. It was true what you saw in the papers about him. Joe is in Baltimore trying to get him release or parole, & Lucy Thirston is trying for the same end so they hope they may succeed—but as

---

[333] An oath of allegiance was to be taken by Southerners.

[334] Testimony of former slaves against whites charged with denying blacks their rights.

[335] Robert Augustus Stiles, son of Uncle Styles (Rev. J. C. Styles) and Caroline Clifford Nephew.

[336] Being held as a prisoner of war.

[337] Anna Catherine King, daughter of William King and Sarah Elizabeth MacLeod.

he will not take the oath, I am afraid he will be sent out of the country. Susie thinks it very probable.

Hatty Tronbridge is going to be married to a Mr. Allen, a very worthy man from N.Y.

I had a visit (my pleasant & comforting it was too) from Brother Jim of two or three days. But he has now returned to Paterson. I am expecting Sister Fanny soon.

Brother Jim says he thinks I did very well to come to Phila, he likes it (as I do) better than N.Y. or Brooklyn.

I saw Mr. McDevitt a few days ago, who spoke with great interest of your dear husband of how much he esteemed him & how deeply he regretted his sad fate.

I have just passed through another sad anniversary, dear Bessie. You better than any one else can understand my feelings. Oh! is it not hard to be thus alone & desolate & in all human probability not more than half life's journey done? But, I earnestly pray for our children's sake, that it may be God's will to spare both you & me, & that we may live to see them grow up to be worthy of their noble fathers. The promise of God to the widow & the fatherless is ever in my heart, & I cannot allow myself to doubt his merciful protection.

I have been in my own house a week now and am almost settled. My furniture is plain, but comfortable—& every thing is very nice. I have two good girls—so far as I can judge, for cook & chamber maid. I hope you will some day come to see me.

The children are pretty well. I am expecting Miss Hamilton[338] next week. Give much love to Mama & father, Nellie,[339] Joe,[340] Aunt Kate,[341] Uncle Pratt[342] & all friends—& write some to

Your own loving sister
Marie R. King.

Address
Walnut St. Below 36th
West Philadephia Pa.

Kiss little Maggie & both the boys for Aunt Marie.

Lexington Georgia
Oct. 20th 1865

Mrs. B.S. King,

Your letter bearing date May 15th (the day I arrived home from Greensboro N.C.) after a circuitous route reached me in the summer bearing signs of having been opened and at this late date I attempt an answer, though I am afriad you will think hard of me for my tardiness— At the time of its reception I was disabled from corresponding by virtue of orders from those in authority here; therefore I hope you will excuse me when I tell you this is my earliest convenience. I have ever made it a rule to leave unanswered no letter and expecially such an one as yours. I regret at this late day to harrow up your feelings by reference to the sad

---

[338] This may be the schoolteacher under whom young Harris King studied during the early years of the war.

[339] Ellen Palmer Stubbs, wife of Joseph Henry King.

[340] Joseph Henry King was a son of Barrington King.

[341] Catherine Barrington King, sister of Barrington King and wife of Rev. Nathaniel A. Pratt.

[342] Rev. Nathaniel A. Pratt.

subject-matter of your letter but it must be. I thank you for so good a letter and the very kind manner in which you allude to the services of my Brother and self. Our reward has been felt in our hearts when we have reflected on the fact that we did as we would be done by. We needed not the profuse expresion of your gratitude that your letter contains, yet we are thankful for it and desire that you should know we appreciate it.

We feel that though one friend is gone another is left to appreciate our kind offices. I am pleased to see from the tone of your letter the spirit of resignation it shows to what does indeed seem a hard and trying dispensation of Gods providence. The conflicts of this life are indeed many and sure but "as thy days so shall thy strength ever be" is a great and consoling promise to mortals in this vale of tears—

—I will give you most cheerfully what further information I may. Brother says that Martin Donarien (of Jefferson County I think) who assisted at the burial[343] took all the things out of his pockets and put them in him (the Cols' haversack) which was by Col Wrights (who was the senior officer) direction taken to his brother Capt. King. Brother knows nothing more concerning them. The ring was left on his hand.[344] Brother says that when they laid him down to rest the expression of his face was natural save that there was a purplish hue on it. Brother saw the memorandum book but did not look in it. If either of us could see you personally we could perhaps give you more satisfaction, and should I ever be in your part of the country will certainly avail myself of your kind invitation to visit the home of my lamented friend. Any other information which I can give will be cheerfully furnished for the asking— Again accept our sincere condolence with and for you & the bereaved "little ones" in this great and

---

[343] Of Barrington S. King.

[344] His wedding ring.

trying affliction, and believe me to be Lady your true friend and sympathiser.

Wiley Chandler Howard[345]

In a letter to his son, Ralph, dated 12 August 1965, Barrington King mentioned the plans to retrieve the body of Barrington Simeral King the following winter.[346] The following letter details the plans for the journey.

Jefferson Jackson County Geo.
December 28th 1865

Mrs Col B.S. King-

Your letter of 20th Inst came to hand, or rather reached Lexington on the 25th, and I proceed immediately to reply. I have changed, as you will see from the caption of this, my place of abode. and am Just entering again the practice of Law. Accept my thanks if on your kind letter, the subject matter of which gives me great concern. Never in-dulge for one moment that. I consider it presumtious in you to make the request contained in your letter, for I am ever ready to contribute, to the extent of my ability, what I can towards the pleasure and happiness of one in your situation It is not asking too much Mrs King, for it is a service that I would gladly render; but the idea of performing so dilicate a service for pay I know not how to entertain and yet the peculiar circumstances surrounding me at present forbid my quieting my business without compensation for last time I am going to be very candid with you. I am a young man commencing

---

[345] Wiley Chandler Howard served as a member of Cobb's Legion, Company C, first lieutenant.

[346] Cooper, *King and Allied Families,* 60.

the business of life a second time with very meager resources; for what little I had *is gone*. *You* will see at once how important for me at this crissis to be at my post, but I have so arranged my affairs as to be able to accompany Capt King,[347] if the Journey can be accomplished by the 20th of January next. If not I can not go till the 7st of ~~March~~ Feb as the 6th is return day for the court here spoken of & as our Superior Court comes off ~~on~~ 26th Feb I have seen my brother since the reception of your letter and it is impossible for him to go. He would gladly go if he could Allowing ten days for me to get a reply from you I could meet Capt King [Ralph King] on the 10th at Union Point as I suppose the route will be by way of Augusta, then we would have ten days to make the journey about the time I calculate it would take If therefore you think it could be so arranged write me at once stateing time & place of meeting & c [etc.]. Write me at this place & I will have the office at Athens watched for the letter as we have no regular office here as yet.

As for compensation for loss of time I can not well tell the value of it and am disposed to leave that to yourself & Capt King after a full hearing had be him from me as to the status of my business. The time has been Mrs King when I would not receive pay for such a service, for really, it ought to be an act, of gratuious kindness, promted along by motives of the purest friendship, whereas to receive pay gives it a different appearance But I trust to believe if I accompany Capt King on this sad mission you & the family will not regard me as a hired man, working for pay; but will understand and appreciate the nobler motive which promps me. Col King was my friend. He has fallen in an heroic defense of his country and the unchanging principles of Justice and right. I am ready and willing to cheerfully perform any service which will contribute to the peace of mind and happiness of his unfortunate and bereaved family. Accept my

---

[347] Captain Ralph Brown King was a brother of Barrington S. King.

brother's, as well as my own best wishes for your future happiness & c.

With sentiments of the highest esteem, I am, Mrs King, as ever, Your true friend—

W. C. Howard[348]

On 17 January 1866, Barrington King, the father of Barrington S. King, died of injuries received when a horse kicked him. He was in the process of rebuilding the Roswell Manufacturing Company with seventy men working for him.

The following letter verifies that Barrington S. King's remains were returned to Roswell, Georgia, from North Carolina during February 1866.

Bushy Park[349] Feb. 20th 1866
Tuesday afternoon-

My Dearest Sister [Bessie]

I have just heard that Cliff[350] arrived in Marietta this morning with dear Brother's precious Remains, and cannot refrain from writing and expressing my *heart-felt* sympathy ~~with~~ for you. in this trying hour. Which it must be an *inexpressible comfort*, it must also be a *great trial*.— But I sincerely hope you will be *strengthened* and *comforted now* and at *all times*, by *Him*. who has *sweetly* promised, *"Never to leave or forsake thee"*— On looking over my scraps of Poetry and few days since, I came across a very touching and beautiful piece called "The *Loved* and *Lost*." I think you will like it, so enclose it to you; please read it

---

[348] Wiley Chandler Howard.

[349] Now known as the Glover-McLeod Garrison House or Rocky Chair Hill at 250 Garrison Road, SE, Marietta GA and is on the National Register of Historical Places. It is a Greek Revival Designed by Willis Ball.

[350] Clifford Alonzo King was the youngest brother of Barrington S. King.

to dear Mrs. King[351]— I'm very sorry that cousin Eva and yourself did not have time to pay us a visit when you came over last week.— Tell cousin Eva that George[352] quite *lost his heart* with *her*; he admired her *very much indeed*. We have been expecting a letter from home for sometime, but it has not come yet. I cannot imagine why some of them don't write; nearly three months have passed since we have received a line a from any of them. George is getting anxious to leave for home, but will not do so until we hear. He wants to pay you a little visit before leaving. How are my little Nephews and Maggie? Every one here thinks *Barrington* your prettiest child. I believe *you* always *insisted* that *he was*. He *is* a *lovely* little darling but not more so than *my little Maggie* I concluded, after thinking the matter over, not to accept Ellen's[353] invitation—to return home with her; did not like the idea of being in any *one's way*— Her engagement, seems to be generally known, so if you feel inclined, may tell Mrs. King and family— How long does Mary King[354] expect to remain in Sav [Savannah]. Grandmother and all unite with me in much love to yourself, Mrs. King, cousin Eva and many kisses to the little ones. May our Heavenly Father watch over and comfort you *now* and *always*, is the earnest prayer of

Your ever loving Sister
Anna C. MacLeod

Once the war ended and soldiers returned home, the frequency of letters decreased. Little is known about the Bessie

---

[351] Bessie's mother-in-law, B. S. King's mother.

[352] George MacLeod, a nephew of Bessie's.

[353] Ellen Palmer Stubbs was the wife of Joseph Henry King, a son of Barrington King.

[354] Mary Eliza Hardee, wife of Clifford Alonzo King.

and the children during this time. Barrington Simeral King's body was brought back to Roswell. Just months after his internment, little Maggie, Catherine Margaret King, the youngest child and only daughter of Barrington Simeral King and Bessie, died 26 May 1866. There is no record of what caused her death. She would have been 1 1/2 years old.

The next recorded activity occurred a year after Maggie died. In this letter we find that Bessie's uncle was overseeing her money and investments, which had previously been the responsibility of Barrington King, her father-in-law, until his death. Interestingly, her uncle refers to her as Bettie.

Savannah May 10th 1867

Dear Bettie [Bessie]

I am perfectly willing to withdraw from the trusteeship, and do hereby give my consent that you have whom you may desire appointed in my stead; I do not know if this my written consent will be sufficient, should anything more be necessary let me know and I will attend to it promptly, as I know it is much better you should have some one with whom you could consult more readily than can be done by letter.

We are all quite well, Ina[355] received your letter about a month after it was written, With love to yourself (in which Ina joins me) and a kiss to the children I remain your

Affectionate Uncle
R.H. McLeod[356]

---

[355] Perhaps the wife of Richard H. MacLeod.

[356] Richard Habersham MacLeod was the paternal uncle of Sarah Elizabeth "Bessie" MacLeod King.

Bessie was not convinced that her money was being managed to the best interest of herself and her children. This trusteeship continued to be passed among the male members of the King family and MacLeod family until Bessie remarried.

Sometime during the early 1870s, Bessie married William Letford.[357] Details of Bessie's life and the lives of the other family members become obscure after the Civil War. The youngest of Bessie's sons, Barrington "Bubba" King, died 26 May 1884 at twenty-two years old of undocumented causes. Harris married Georgia Baker and continued to write his mother regularly regarding his wife, their children, and his business in Savannah.

---

[357] William Letford was born in 1840 and was living in Savannah GA in 1870. He served in the 20th Infantry, Company B, in the Confederate Army.

BIBLIOGRAPHY

Boatner, Mark Mayo, III. *The Civil War Dictionary*. Revised edition. New York: David McKay Company, Inc., 1988.

Capers Battalion Georgia Militia. <www.researchonline.net/gaew/unit140.htm>.

Coleman, Richard G. *A Short History of the Roswell Manufacturing Company of Roswell, Georgia: Home of "Roswell Grey."* N.p, 1982.

Cooper, Sarah Joyce King. *King and Allied Families*. Athens GA: Agee Publishers, Inc., 1992.

Crute, Joseph H., Jr. *Units of the Confederate States Army*. Midlothian VA: Derwent Books, 1987.

Dillman, Caroline Matheny. *Days Gone By in Alpharetta and Roswell Georgia*. First edition. Roswell GA: Chattahoochee Press, 1992.

Evans, Clement. *Confederate Military History*. Volume 3. Atlanta: Confederate Publishing Company, 1899.

Hewett, Janet B., editor. *The Roster of Confederate Soldiers, 1861–1865*. Wilmington NC: Broadfoot Publishing Company, 1995.

Martin, Clarece. *A History of Roswell Presbyterian Church*. Dallas: Taylor Publishing Company, 1984.

SC State House History. <www.scstatehouse.net-LPITR>.

Skinner, Arthur N. and James L. Skinner, editors. *The Death of a Confederate: Selections from the Letters of the Archibald Smith Family of Roswell, Georgia, 1864–1956*. Athens: University of Georgia Press, 1996.

Smedlund, William S. *Camp Fires of Georgia's Troops, 1861–1865*. Lithonia GA: Kennesaw Mountain Press, 1994.

US Bureau of the Census. *1860 Census of Population*. Washington, DC: Government Printing Office.

The War of the Rebellion: A Compilation of the Official Records of the Union and Confederate Armies. Washington, DC: Government Printing Office, 1880–1902.

Webster's New Twentieth Century Dictionary of the English Language. Unabridged. Second edition. New York: The World Publishing Company, 1971.

Williams' Atlanta City Directory for 1859–1860. Atlanta: M. Lynch, 1859.

INDEX

Tyler, John 59

'Uncle Pratt. See Pratt, Reverend
  Nathaniel Alpheus.
Uncle Styles. See Styles, Joseph
  Clay.
Union Point, GA 134
United States House of
  Representatives 36
United State Senate 36
Upperville, VA Battle of,
  Gettysburg Campaign 29

variola 65
varioloid 65
Vaughn, Claborn 34, 43, 47, 49,
  54
Vickery Creek, GA 1, 3
Vicksburg, Battle of 28, 55, 57
Virginia 18, 47, 85, 97, 118
Virginia Battery, CSA 68
Virginia Central Railroad 65, 68
Virginia Infantry, CSA 39
Virginia Military Institute 48
Voss, James A. 24, 43
Voss, Rebecca 43

Waddel, Dr. 41
Walker, W. S. 25
Walters, W. T. 127
Waring, J. Frederick 19
Washington, DC 32, 46, 64, 116
Waterloo Bridge, VA 121
Waynesboro, VA, Shenandoah
  Valley Campaign of Sheridan
  91
Webb, Bryce 25
Weigle, G. 72
West Point 18, 32
Wheeler, Joseph "Fighting Joe"
  106
White's Battalion, CSA 67
Wickham's Brigade, CSA 67

Wilderness Campaign 6, 38-39,
  50, 59
Willbanks, M. A. 42
Willbanks, Richard H. 42-43
Williams, Thomas H. 21, 117, 120
Williams, William M. 21
Williamsburg Road, VA 97
Williamsport, VA 28
Wilmington, NC 113, 115
Winchester, VA, Gettysburg
  Campaign 45
Windsor, Connecticut 1
Withers, John 52
Woodruff, Berrimon 25-26
woolen mill 4, 51, 77
Wright, Daniel 42
Wright, Gilbert J. 19, 63, 75, 111,
  122, 132
Wright, M. H. 51
Wright, M. J. 103

Yancey, Benjamin C. 19
yankees 34-37, 40, 44-45, 48, 56,
  61-62, 64, 69-70, 72, 74, 80-
  82, 84-85, 88-89, 91, 92, 100,
  102, 104, 110-111, 113, 115,
  121
yarn 87, 93, 99, 111, 113
Yellow Tavern, VA, Sherdian's
  Richmond Raid 39, 45
Yobel, slave 102
Yorktown, VA, Peninsular
  Campaign 6
Yorktown, VA 19
Young, Pierce Manning Butler 18-
  19, 30, 44, 46, 66, 67, 120
Young, William 42
Young's Brigade 67, 103, 109,
  121